I0436285

Editor-in-Chief and Founder:
  Lyndon H. LaRouche, Jr.
Editorial Board: *Lyndon H. LaRouche, Jr. , Helga
  Zepp-LaRouche, Robert Ingraham, Tony
  Papert, Gerald Rose, Dennis Small, Jeffrey
  Steinberg, William Wertz*
Co-Editors: *Robert Ingraham, Tony Papert*
Managing Editor: *Nancy Spannaus*
Technology: *Marsha Freeman*
Books: *Katherine Notley*
Ebooks: *Richard Burden*
Graphics: *Alan Yue*
Photos: *Stuart Lewis*
Circulation Manager: *Stanley Ezrol*

INTELLIGENCE DIRECTORS
Counterintelligence: *Jeffrey Steinberg, Michele
  Steinberg*
Economics: *John Hoefle, Marcia Merry Baker,
  Paul Gallagher*
History: *Anton Chaitkin*
Ibero-America: *Dennis Small*
Russia and Eastern Europe: *Rachel Douglas*
United States: *Debra Freeman*

INTERNATIONAL BUREAUS
Bogotá: *Miriam Redondo*
Berlin: *Rainer Apel*
Copenhagen: *Tom Gillesberg*
Houston: *Harley Schlanger*
Lima: *Sara Madueño*
Melbourne: *Robert Barwick*
Mexico City: *Gerardo Castilleja Chávez*
New Delhi: *Ramtanu Maitra*
Paris: *Christine Bierre*
Stockholm: *Ulf Sandmark*
United Nations, N.Y.C.: *Leni Rubinstein*
Washington, D.C.: *William Jones*
Wiesbaden: *Göran Haglund*

ON THE WEB
e-mail: eirns@larouchepub.com
www.larouchepub.com
www.executiveintelligencereview.com
www.larouchepub.com/eiw
Webmaster: *John Sigerson*
Assistant Webmaster: *George Hollis*
Editor, Arabic-language edition: *Hussein Askary*

EIR (ISSN 0273-6314) *is published weekly
(50 issues), by EIR News Service, Inc.,
P.O. Box 17390, Washington, D.C. 20041-0390.
(703) 777-9451*

European Headquarters: E.I.R. GmbH, Postfach
Bahnstrasse 9a, D-65205, Wiesbaden, Germany
Tel: 49-611-73650
Homepage: http://www.eirna.com
e-mail: eirna@eirna.com
Director: Georg Neudecker

Montreal, Canada: 514-461-1557

Denmark: EIR - Danmark, Sankt Knuds Vej 11,
basement left, DK-1903 Frederiksberg, Denmark.
Tel.: +45 35 43 60 40, Fax: +45 35 43 87 57. e-mail:
eirdk@hotmail.com.

Mexico City: EIR, Sor Juana Inés de la Cruz 242-2
Col. Agricultura C.P. 11360
Delegación M. Hidalgo, México D.F.
Tel. (5525) 5318-2301
eirmexico@gmail.com

Canada Post Publication Sales Agreement
#40683579

Postmaster: Send all address changes to *EIR*, P.O.
Box 17390, Washington, D.C. 20041-0390.

Signed articles in *EIR* represent the views of the
authors, and not necessarily those of the Editorial
Board.

The Moral Fitness
To Survive

Emergency Action Now

Feb. 14—Lyndon LaRouche spoke to associates today to this effect.

You're looking at a general, sudden collapse of the economy of the United States, and of Europe in general.

Right now, the situation is that the entire trans-Atlantic community is bankrupt, hopelessly bankrupt. And there's no escape from it; everything is going down in bankruptcy unless someone comes along and re-organizes the whole system.

We have the ability to shut down Wall Street now, because the feeling of panic in Wall Street is so acute that they will do anything to survive. But they won't survive, however. They can't survive. They'll just be gone.

What I see is a highly probable case of the withdrawal of Obama from the office of the Presidency. If someone in the Congress, especially the Senate, really gets on this thing, they have the power to make decisions which would secure the United States from a catastrophic collapse. If there are people, and I believe there are inside the United States, who take that view that I do,— what we would do, is we would go to members of the Congress, especially the Senate, and we would then operate on the basis of shutting this whole thing down, based on a statement that the system is bankrupt, and therefore there has to be an immediate U.S. action, which is a Presidential action essentially. We will suspend the current President, taking emergency action in defiance of this President,

Shut down Wall Street now!

in order to bring forth a group of people mostly from Congressional circles, especially the Senate. And if we get some people in the Senate and some others to agree on this thing, we can save the United States from bankruptcy.

That's the real option we need to grab for. I certainly know how to do that, and I'm sure other people also have those talents.

We're on the edge of the sudden collapse of civilization, and what we do is crucial.

EIR Contents

www.larouchepub.com Volume 43, Number 8, February 19, 2016

Cover This Week

Russian President Vladimir Putin

Presidential Press and Information Office

Corrections: The following corrections are for our Feb. 12, 2016 issue. In "China's Mission to Lunar Far Side Opens New Frontier for Mankind" (p. 6), the opening quotation from President John F. Kennedy was originally part of his announcement of the program to put a man on the Moon in his address to a special joint session of Congress on May 25, 1961, and is cited in that context. The diagram of a halo orbit around the Earth-Moon L2 point (p. 7) is conceptually correct, but the dimensions indicated in the diagram should be disregarded. The photograph of President Kennedy (p. 9) is properly captioned, "President John F. Kennedy, Glenn Seaborg, and Harry Finger on a tour of the Jackass Flats, Nevada test site, where work on the NERVA nuclear rocket engine was underway."

In "How America's Space Program Has Been Nearly Destroyed" (p. 17), the caption of the photo of President Kennedy should indicate that he announced the Apollo program before the 1961 special joint session of Congress, and called for landing a man on the Moon "before this decade is out." On p. 21, the photo shows Apollo 15's Jim Irwin on the Moon, saluting the American flag.

Prometheus in the Twenty-First Century

These are edited excerpts from Lyndon LaRouche's dialogue with the LaRouche PAC Policy Committee on Feb. 8.

Host Matthew Ogden: You have a quadrupling of the NATO expansion, the troop presence, and the advanced hardware on Russia's border. You have the admission by top leading economists in Europe that this entire economic system is on the verge of disintegrating, and people are even talking about a debt jubilee,— cancelling the debt. And you've got the fact that there's a very clear recognition of your leadership when it comes to shutting down Wall Street and reinstating the full Franklin Roosevelt program.

Lyndon Larouche: One of my favorite sports. [laughter] It's become that. I didn't intend that to happen, but it did happen. Despite all my fervid intentions not to do that. But it is of that nature.

We have to understand a lot of things, but most of all, we have to understand exactly what the world is like. Because what's happening now is that most of the nations which are trans-Atlantic nations, are actually in the mud right now. They're not performing well; quite the contrary.

The options are concentrated largely in Russia, China, and their immediate friends. The British Empire is the cause of this general problem which the whole planet has been going through for a very long time,— that's the thing that's dangerous, and that's the thing we've got to destroy.

But then in the process of destruction, we've got to try to see how many parts of the human species can be rescued from this. You take, for example, California and the population of California, including the students and the young people. In general, they've been destroyed, and the youth especially. And therefore, we recognize that China, Russia, and a few others, are well-organized to accomplish something, whatever the difficulties may be that they run into. But the point is that the United States, its people, the Americas in general,— they are actually in a degenerated condition, and other parts of the world are also, with people who are running away from parts of the planet, dying at a great rate, great batches,— all these things. Therefore, I think what's interesting for us, is that we do know what is happening in terms of the Eurasian area, the Eurasian population is progressive.

The drive is against that from Europe, or from the trans-Atlantic area; and therefore, our problem is, we

President Franklin Roosevelt delivers a fireside chat to the nation.

NASA/JPL-Caltech

Self-portrait of the Mars Rover Curiosity, surrounded by the tracks of its wheels, with Mars' Mount Sharp in the background. Curiosity took the photos for this composite image on Oct. 31 and Nov. 1, 2012.

have to on the one hand, make sure that this one factor, the Eurasian factor, that that is kept as protected. And then we've got to put the leverage on to cure the other parts of the planet, which are in terrible and deteriorating condition, accelerating rates of degeneration. And so, these I think are two of the practical questions: What is good? What can be good? And what is very bad, and could be worse?. . . .

Kesha Rogers of Houston, Texas: I would start from what Lyn presented last night to members of the organization (lead editorial of *EIR* No.7), in terms of the discussion we had, from the standpoint of FDR as the image of leadership, because most of the population has no conception of what the idea of a productive society looks like. And this gets to the heart of the flaw in education, the corruption of our education system. It gets to the heart of what has been done in the takedown of our space program.

But I think that what should really be emphasized throughout, is that what you're fighting for is the defense of the human mind. That's what's being targeted right now. And yet most people look at the space program as just a thing in and of itself, to protect certain programs, or so that people who have certain specialties will get money for their specialties, over other specialties.

But once again, a national mission has to start with a higher conception of the fight for the human mind. And this is something that Mr. LaRouche has been addressing,— you have been addressing— for quite some time, from the standpoint of: Look at what we have done in terms of our ability with, say, the Mars Curiosity mission, that everyone got extremely excited about. This showed a new direction for mankind. And China is developing it even further, from the standpoint of the idea that the extended sensory apparatus of the mind of man would be able to go out into the distances of space, without particularly having to send human beings there. But you have a different conception of what these instruments are, and what are the data that it's bringing back, showing to the population how it is actually bettering our understanding as human beings of the universe that we live in.

One thing that I really want to put a focal point on, from the standpoint of the fight to defend NASA, is first of all, that we have lost touch with the idea of what NASA represents in terms of a fight to really protect the identity of the human mind, and what it really is supposed to represent.

I'm reading about and investigating a powerful lady by the name of Henrietta Leavitt. And I've mentioned her before. There's not a whole lot of work out there about her. There's a book called, *Miss Leavitt's Stars*. The idea is that she gets to this very point. She was a lady who was really spectacular in her discovery, because her discovery was not made from the standpoint of sending humans out into space, but from the standpoint of how far the mind can go, and how much the mind can discover, from the standpoint of understanding relationships. She made the discovery that by mea-

Henrietta Swan Leavitt at her desk in the Harvard College Observatory.

suring the brightness and the period of pulsating stars we could determine the distances of stars and galaxies that later led to the overturning of the prevailing notion that our galaxy, the Milky Way, was the only galaxy out there, which was not true. And her discoveries helped us to better understand that.

But more, her discoveries helped us to understand that we have a lot to learn about the universe we live in, and that only the human mind can help us to make that discovery. And that's just an example of what we can accomplish with the space program. And it also is an example of the fact that China is committed to doing that, and we can use that as an example, and get the United States back on that track. But once again, there has to be a national mission, and it has to be a mission centered around that type of identity.

The Two Systems Can't Coexist

LaRouche: In practice the area which is controlled, largely by Russia and China, and the nations which are now coming together grouped around them, are the only thing of any significance in a group or large-scale significance, which is going to do any good for mankind.

In a sense, what you have to get rid of, is the trans-Atlantic community. Now, that doesn't mean you're going to eliminate the people, but it means you're going to eliminate their habit. And that's the only way you're going to do it. As a matter of fact, the only way you can get a healthy population on this planet is by crushing what we have in the trans-Atlantic region. You've got to clean it up! You can talk and say, well, are we going to help cure people of their disease? How can you cure a

person, when their life is based on their disease? And that's the point.

You get things in Germany, for example. You have a complicated state of mind among the German population, because the German population is one of the least diseased in particular, of the trans-Atlantic community. There are reasons for that, but there also are reasons because the Germans were treated as pariahs on the basis of the Hitler phenomenon. It was just an arbitrary thing.

The French system is a system that's rotten to the core! Yes, there are people there who are decent people among the French, but the system stinks! It's evil! And it spreads the evil, it's spread it into Germany! That's how the evil got back into Germany: It came by way of the British, the British by way of the French.

So the French system is one of the chief instruments for the destruction of the minds of people in the trans-Atlantic community, especially in Europe. And you see this all over the place.

So, we are going to have to actually,— not wait and say "cure people of their bad habits,"— that kind of thing, as we know from experience, doesn't work very well. When people get into bad habits, they generally defend the bad habits first. And they comment on the subject afterward. No! We are in a situation where we are ready for a global war. That doesn't mean it's going to happen that way; it means that the condition of life in the trans-Atlantic community has reached such a nature, which is a British-dominated nature. It's British; and that's Satanic.

So we're in a situation where we are going to come to something which is tantamount to the edge of a war, a general war throughout the planet. Because you cannot have the two systems coexisting. You cannot have the kind of system that the British Empire represents in the trans-Atlantic community, at the same time that you're trying to rebuild an economy in Eurasia. So the conflict is going to be very tough. Perhaps even disastrous. But that's where we are right now. . . .

A New System for Mankind

LaRouche: Let's take the case of the decline and fall of the Roman Empire: What we're looking at is a phenomenon very much like that, which is happening throughout the trans-Atlantic area. What we saw in the case of the Roman Empire was that this thing never cures itself. It was always evil. It was never purified. Only population reduction resulting from its policies made the disease of the empire less manifest.

We're now in a situation which is comparable to the fall of the Roman Empire. What is the Roman Empire? Well, implicitly it's the trans-Atlantic community, and the trans-Atlantic community is ready to go to Hell. And the point is, don't worry about that, don't try to save it. If you try to save the Roman Empire,— if you read the Roman legacies and so forth, you find that didn't work very well at all. They got killed!

Therefore, the point is, you're going to get an extermination of a policy, a mental case of outlook, which is going to be comparable to the decline of the Roman Empire. And as I say, the British Empire is the new Roman Empire, and the problem is that the British Empire, which includes the United States, still does mean the United States!

That's what's happened to the United States; it happened immediately with the beginning of the United States as a nation. The destruction was massive: most of the Presidents of the United States were actually enemies of the United States; most of them were! And that's why the problem keeps coming back, and still does. This is the Roman Empire, the Roman Empire model.

And you've got the Eurasian model now, the resuscitation of China, and what Putin has done on his part. He was inspired on this thing. Remember, as I've mentioned a number of times, his family, Putin's family came from an area which was a concentration of death, because of the location of the battles there [Leningrad, now St. Petersburg]. And Putin has managed to be a factor in bringing about a strengthening of both China *and* Russia, to save Russia. And examine what the implications are; and what I've seen from the areas I used to poke around in, you know, in India and so forth, areas which I was working in.

And what we're seeing is that this area, this Eurasian area contains within it elements which are the basis of creating or recreating a new system for mankind. And what the result will be,— the characteristic built into this thing, the characteristic is, the space pro-

The last Roman Emperor, Romulus Augustus, reigned 475 to 476, when he was deposed by Odoacer, who called himself King of Italy. Here, a coin issued by the teenaged Romulus.

gram.

What do we mean by the space program? Well, not the space program the way the idiot thinks about the space program, but the space program as a reflection of the fact that mankind is getting wise. With the new Chinese far-side-of-the-Moon operation, mankind is getting wise to the reality that mankind on Earth is not the power that rules Earth; but rather, there is a force beyond that, which controls the achievement of space, and that means that mankind is a creature that *lives* in space. And it's in that area, that domain, and the activities and development in that domain, which is the future for mankind.

The important thing here is, you have to just take a little, short trip and think about it. What does this mean? And right now, the new Moon project is probably the key to bringing this idea not only into what's happening in China right now, but for the entire human species. But we're going for a change in the *species characteristics*, from what had been traditional and what is going to emerge, now, from the new change.

And so therefore, the idea, if you want to do something good, look at that. Don't ask what somebody says, "well, I think that that is this; I think that that is that . . ." That's no good! The problem is that mankind has been a failure, but why has mankind been a failure? Not because of mankind's inherent nature. But because of his corruption. . . .

Mankind Has To Change

LaRouche: Einstein. Einstein was a unique figure in history during his generation. He was unique. That is, the scientists around him were failures, and those who would follow in the footsteps of those failures, are still failures; and they've become worse failures than they were before.

So mankind has to change. This is the thing I keep reminding people, from time to time,— that mankind has a mission in the Universe, and it does not lie in some local area or some local scheme. It's like a harvesting process, that mankind is able to find in their own hands,— like they have the right seeds, and get the right seeds in the process, and then the process of natural development of mankind proceeds, as being located within the Solar system. Now, that's not an extraordinary thing; it's true! And Einstein is an example of exactly what that means,— that is, his record, his legacy represents that. What was the difference with Einstein, what was the difference?

Well, you've got two cases of his categorical discoveries, that these things introduce something. Then he died. Well, I don't know who to blame for his dying; but the problem is, his approach to *science* was killed! And you have people who are actually decent scientists, but they're *stuck* on the implications of this thing.

And we have a mission, and to me the mission is very clear: We've got to get rid of the legacy which we cling to, like desperate people. And you have to understand that what people say is "practical" is what is evil. You want a definition of evil? Be practical! ...

Albert Einstein in 1921

a person who has been generating creativity for mankind. And therefore, Einstein is very important for this, because here's a man who's an example by his life, by his work,— and he was a creative person. What did he create? He created people! Well, didn't they already live? Yes! But what was the difference with the ones that worked with him? Under his influence, they're quite different! Mankind is not waiting for birth out there, as such. Mankind is waiting to discover what mankind already has.

The idea is that the human individual is able to create a power of creativity in the human being! And that's not something that dumps on you; that's something that comes from the process of your existence. And if you can achieve that progress, that's the proof of creativity. And the idea,— the creativity which lies beyond the past,— that is what the truth is.

They Want an Explanation

LaRouche: You can use the term "God," but I think that when people use those terms, they get trapped into a misunderstanding of what the whole meaning is. Look, what's the nature of mankind? What makes mankind different than any animal, what? Unique. What is it? It's the power of creativity.

Now, what is this power of creativity? This can be expressed in a child's mind, in the question of the development of that mind. Because in the course of mankind, each generation of humanity should be making an original contribution to the future of mankind. And that's the intention here. So people say, "God will do this, God will do that." Wait a minute, buddy! Who's this "God" that you're talking about? I mean, anybody that you know, personally, that you have worked with personally on this thing? Of course not!

The problem is, they want to come out with an "explanation." They want to create an image, an image of a Creator in whose existence they don't believe. That is, they don't believe in it in practice. Because they are not

People say we're going to inherit this, we're going to inherit that— no. Mankind as a species, develops within the body of mankind, the aptitude of creating creativity beyond anything that any living mind has heretofore done: the creativity of the individual.

And it's when you understand *this*, which has been my particular emphasis,— that's what makes the difference. The human species is the only species we know of, which can voluntarily create a new state in the universe.

All this other stuff, this substitute, "Oh this is my explanation, my explanation, this is my opinion."... It's nonsense! The question is, mankind is unique in the Solar system, in the system as we know it. Mankind is unique, and the point is, if you don't get your children to grow up a little bit and become smarter and so forth, then you're working for Satan. We have a lot of those, like Trump, for example. [laughter]

Michael Steger of San Francisco: Well, Lyn, implicitly, you've just taken the discussion to the area of what is your unique contribution to this whole idea, which is to make clear in a more scientific way the role of Classical music and composition in shaping the question of scientific thought in the human mind. It was understood, but yet really hadn't been made conscious; maybe you have more to say. But that seems to be where we've taken the discussion now.

The Baby Genius

LaRouche: It can be taken further, obviously,— that's presumably an approximation. But no, the idea of mankind, *inherently* — inherently — within mankind, within the body of mankind, of people, mankind; that is where the creativity lies. You get a little baby started, and the baby functions, and the baby becomes a little genius as they call it; and you say, that is a creative force, that kind of creativity in the individual human being, as from a child, from a very young child who is fortunate enough to be able to develop a real force of creativity. You take the greatest, most creative people we know of in history, and they stand out for that.

Kepler's an example of that. Kepler's a perfect example of that. And so, he was a genius; he died on the field of battle, but he wasn't fighting. He was just not getting fed; those were the conditions he was living under. But his discovery was unique! What he discovered on the question of the Solar system was unique! What we should be looking for is those things which are unique acts of creativity, and the promotion of them, and the development of the appreciation of them!

And that's where the weakness lies, that we don't do that. We want an explanation, like a ready-made explanation. We don't have the force inside us to force ourselves to create something which is an absolutely new idea, which never came to any other person before. *Never!* And that's what you're looking for. And Einstein is a model of this kind of existence.

Megan Beets of the LaRouche PAC Science Team: If you go back to what you brought up in the beginning about education, and you were just referencing the child, you're really discussing a process of play, of creative play; and in the child it takes one form, and in the adult it takes a slightly different form, which is what you're saying, the creation of something new which has never occurred before.

LaRouche: Well, I've had children, and I've

Prometheus carries fire in this painting by Seventeenth-century Flemish artist Jan Cossiers.

watched this, and I've watched people at an earlier age in this sort of thing, and I've seen it. We used to get fascinated by babies, you know, young babies, because you would see them doing something like that; you would see them doing something which was absolutely original; they would look at something and they would discover something. It was often silly, and this and that, but it was unique! And the very fact that it was something new which the child created—the parents didn't do that, the child did; or the environment for the child. And therefore, this process in mankind which is unique *to* mankind, is the real principle of humanity.

And when people don't do that, they fall out of the category of being useful. But this process,— the universe obeys the principle, which is the same principle.

The universe behaves according to that principle; that's how the whole system works anyway. Without that it doesn't work!

Diane Sare of Manhattan: You know, in music, they go to great lengths to *dis*courage creativity, and there's also a great deal of confusion people have today between creativity and what they call "innovation." But I was just thinking, Furtwängler discussing why people love certain symphonies, where there's clearly a quality of Beethoven's *Fifth Symphony* or *Ninth Symphony*, or certain pieces that have survived hundreds of years, and others that have fallen by the wayside; so that even in a dark age, there's something which is recognized as a certain unique quality which is accessible to the human population.

LaRouche: Well, I think mankind has never, generally, with some rare exceptions, understood the truth about mankind. They always say, "the baby was born" or so forth, and that was what did it; but that wasn't what did it. It was a process, because the baby being born is a vehicle which may be a source within mankind as a community, of the development of the creative powers. And it's the creative powers of the human mind which distinguish mankind from all other known living creatures.

Rachel Brinkley of Boston: And so, history which seems to be a continuous process to many is more like Planck and Einstein would have viewed it, that there are characteristic changes, like supernovae, which actually are important; it's the burst of activity, not the continuous wave of activity which actually defines the process.

LaRouche: That's the idea of having children, you know. The real motive of that. That since you have not produced enough creativity, yourself, go have a baby, and make sure that that baby makes an accidental discovery or what appears to be an accidental discovery; and you watch this child, and you say, "this kid's smarter than I am!" [laughter]

This is the way it all works! You see it, I mean,

Bust of Filippo Brunelleschi in the Museo dell'Opera del Duomo, Florence.
Wikimedia

you'll see it; a child coming in and making a statement which is actually a statement of a discovery that the child's mind has made! That's the fun.

So the question of creativity means that the whole system of the Solar system and beyond, is essentially dominated by these events, the same events which are the events who are characterized *by* the system, as a whole. It's there! The question is, what do you want to do? You want to create people who are creative. You want to be able to create babies, which are themselves creative in an original way. And you see that: Einstein was, for example, a good example of this,— if you take what we know of his history,— that human creativity is a unique matter; it is what really should dominate and control the history of mankind.

And the problem is we then try to play around with games and tricks; it doesn't work. Einstein was against Satan. That's the issue; it was Einstein. Oh, he's the guy who that hated Satan,— taught him algebra.

Filippo Brunelleschi

Rogers: That is an interesting image, though, that you painted on this question of the baby being born as the source of creativity, because if you think about,— it puts a whole different conception on the idea of, for instance, not just the human born child, but, I would say, the Baby Jesus. And that being a real source of,— what is this idea of creativity that has been given to mankind? And I don't have a full idea about it, but that was just something I was thinking about, when you said that; and it brings forth this conception of looking at what Cusa was thinking about in his investigations from that standpoint in the *De Docta Ignorantia* [*Learned Igorance.* 1440]. But that's the first conception that came to my mind when you were saying that: Is this idea of this conception of the creativity from the standpoint of Christ being born into humanity and bringing forth this idea of what is the access of creativity to humanity?

10   Moral Fitness To Survive

EIR   February 19, 2016

LaRouche: Take the case of Brunelleschi. Now, Brunelleschi was actually a unique person. And the discoveries that were made by him. He made them! And the people who were supposedly his rivals would sit there, foaming at the mouth, or something like that, and they would just sit there, because they couldn't make an invention.

Now, we know that in the course of history there are people who seem to be unique in their ability to make these kinds of discoveries, that is discoveries of new principles, as opposed to the application of a known principle. Education at its best is the development of a known discovery of principle. But there are some people who are a little more creative and actually made creative discoveries as a matter of character. He was that: Brunelleschi.

And you see, the Renaissance comes out of Brunelleschi, the Renaissance as it emerged. There were earlier forms of Renaissance. So what happens is, you find one person, like Brunelleschi who made greater discoveries than anyone in his lifetime, and from earlier! And there were people like that, in a similar way in earlier parts of history, the knowable people.

So what you should search for is those kinds of cases where people do become original creators, and you want to understand *how* that works. And you may not make a discovery, but the discovery may make you. And that's the principle. You want a creation of people who can be creative.

The other side of course, is the fact of what is evil. Obama is pure evil. You know, what're you going to do? Get rid of him: He's evil. He is Satanic, explicitly Satanic. So therefore, the question is we've got to eliminate Satanic influences inside our society.

I think Trump is a failure as Satanic. He's nasty, he's got all the disgusting characteristics you could possibly want. And yet, he's only a Trump. He steals a lot, tries to steal. But I think he has to beg more often than steal.

This is the thing I keep saying repeatedly on these occasions: What is the nature of mankind? And mankind is a creative force unto itself; it is not something else. And the object is to get an environment in which you get more people who are actually truly creative. How do you do that? By protecting them as much as possible from the bastards who try to mold them. And our job is to do as much as we can to contribute to that process.

Vladimir Putin and the New Hope for Mankind

by Robert Ingraham

Feb. 13—Satanically gleeful, with bugged-out eyes and flapping arms, on Oct. 20, 2011 during an interview with CBS news, then Secretary of State Hillary Clinton, upon hearing of the sadistic torture and murder of Libyan President Muammar Qaddafi, gushed out in an orgasm of ecstacy, *"We came, we saw, he died."*[1]

It is now known that Mrs. Clinton's master, Barack Obama, has carried out ten times more drone strikes than those ordered by his White House predecessor George W. Bush. Obama has killed at least 5,000 people, of whom 90-95% have been innocent men, women, and children. And these figures do not include the more than 1,000 drone attacks in Afghanistan.

This is a dark age, where murder is celebrated with triumphalism. It is bestiality. It is human depravity. It is a dying empire, lashing out, killing, spreading chaos, destroying cultures—all in a futile attempt to save itself. As Lyndon LaRouche described the current state of humanity, in a dialogue on Feb. 8, 2016[2]:

> Well, let's take the case of the Roman Empire, the decline and fall of the Roman Empire, and

kremlin.ru

The first formal summit of the BRIC nations (before South Africa joined) was held on June 16, 2009 in Yekaterinburg, Russia. This summit led to the formation of the BRICS Forum, ultimately leading to the decision to create an alternative global financial institution to end IMF dominance.

what we're looking at is a phenomenon very much like that, which is happening throughout the trans-Atlantic area. Now therefore, what happened, as we saw in the case of the Roman Empire, this thing never cured itself. It was always evil. And what happened is, it was never purified, except that some of the people were removed, by being reduced. So therefore, the disease was less manifest.

> What we're in now, is a situation which is comparable to the fall of the Roman Empire. That is, the entire area, remember the Roman Empire: What is the Roman Empire? Well, implicitly it's the trans-Atlantic community, and the trans-Atlantic community is ready to go to Hell. And the point is, is don't worry about that, don't try to save it. If you try to save the Roman Empire, if you read the Roman legacies and so forth, you find that didn't work very well at all. They got killed!

> The point is, you're going to get an extermination of a policy, a mental case of outlook, which is going to be comparable to the decline of the Roman Empire. And as I say, the British Empire is the new Roman Empire, and the problem is that the British Empire, which includes the United States, still does mean the United States!

---

1. If you have the stomach, you can watch it at https://www.youtube.com/watch?v=FgcdIghag5Y

2. See https://larouchepac.com/20160208/lpac-policy-committee-show-february-8-2016

That's what's happened to the United States; it happened immediately, with the beginning of the United States as a nation. The destruction was massive: most of the Presidents of the United States were actually enemies of the United States; most of them were! And that's why the problem keeps coming back. And still does: This is the Roman Empire, the Roman Empire model.

I. The Way Out

On June 16, 2009 the first formal summit of the BRICS[3] nations was held at Yekaterinburg, Russia. This event had been preceded by negotiations going back to an original meeting of foreign ministers held in New York City in 2006. The Yekaterinburg summit was followed by the creation of the BRICS Forum in 2011, and at the fifth BRICS summit in 2013 a decision was reached to create a global financial institution which would liberate these nations from financial subservience to the trans-Atlantic dominated IMF and World Bank. In September 2013 an agreement was finalized at a meeting of BRICS leaders in St. Petersburg for the creation of a $100 billion development bank, with China contributing $41 billion; Brazil, India, and Russia $18 billion each; and South Africa $5 billion.

On July 15, 2014 the sixth BRICS summit convened at Fortaleza, Brazil, where the leaders of the BRICS nations signed the documents to create the $100 billion New Development Bank and simultaneously establish a reserve currency pool worth another $100 billion. Various documents on economic cooperation and development projects were also signed.

Even prior to these developments, on June 15, 2001 representatives of Russia, China, Kyrgyzstan, Kazakhstan, Tajikistan, and Uzbekistan, at a meeting in Shanghai, China issued the *Declaration of Shanghai Cooperation Organization*, establishing the Shanghai Cooperation Organization as a body committed to pursuing cooperation, regional security, economic and scientific development, and defending national sovereignty. One month later, on July 16, Russian President Vladimir Putin and Chinese Premier Jiang Zemin, in Moscow, signed the bilateral *Treaty of Good-Neighborliness and Friendly Cooperation*, a twenty-year strategic treaty between the two nations which commits them

___
3. That is, Brazil, Russia, India, China, South Africa.

to friendship and in-depth partnership in economic, military, diplomatic, and scientific spheres. A selected clause defines the intent of the treaty: to *"endeavor to enhance relations between the two countries to a completely new level, determined to develop the friendship between the people of the two countries from generation to generation...."*

Half of Humanity

In July 2005 a watershed was reached when India, Iran, Mongolia, and Pakistan all attended an SCO summit for the first time. At that meeting, Nursultan Nazarbayev, the President of Kazhkstan, greeted the guests in words that had never before been uttered: "The leaders of the states sitting at this negotiation table are representatives of half of humanity." By 2007 the SCO had initiated dozens of large-scale projects related to transportation, energy, and telecommunications, establishing a paradigm which would then be further advanced with the 2009 founding of the BRICS and the subsequent announcement by Xi Jinping of the "One Belt, One Road" policy in September 2013.

These developments all flow from the 2001 collaboration between Vladimir Putin and the Chinese leadership, and all were made possible by the 2001 *Treaty of Good-Neighborliness*. As the trans-Atlantic world—now dominated by cannibalization of its productive capabilities and a crashing imperial financial system, fractures and crashes like the Roman Empire, more than half of humanity has now vowed to build a better world of economic development and human opportunity. Short of an Obama/House of Windsor provoked World War III, this is the hoped for future for mankind.

II. Enter Vladimir Putin

To quote again from Lyndon LaRouche's Feb. 8 dialogue:

> And what you've got, you've got the Eurasian model now, the resuscitation of China; what Putin has done on his part. He was inspired on this thing. Remember, as I've mentioned a number of times, his family, Putin's family came from an area which was a concentration of death, because of the location of the battles there. And Putin has managed to be a factor in bringing about a strengthening, of both China *and* Russia,

Russian State TV

Russian President Boris Yeltsin resigned Dec. 31, 1999, handing over power to Prime Minister Vladimir Putin. In 1996. Yeltsin had signed a humiliating treaty with terrorists in Chechnya.

Russian State TV

In August 1999, after Chechnyan terrorists invaded the Russian province of Dagestan, Putin went to the front lines and delivered a legendary toast to military commanders, stating that he and they would not drink the vodka toast until the crucial task was completed.

to save Russia. And what the implications are; and what I've seen from the areas I used to poke around in, you know, in India and so forth, areas which I was working in.

And what we're seeing is that this area, this Eurasian area contains within it, elements which are the basis of creating or recreating a new system for mankind. And what the result will be, the characteristic built into this thing, the characteristic is, the space program.

By 1999 the Russian nation was at the point of disappearing. This is not a mere figure of speech. Many people talked openly about the impending "Yugoslavization" of Russia.[4] Not the dismemberment of the already disappeared Soviet Union, but of Russia itself. During the Yeltsin years of the 1990s, Russia had been stripped bare and looted by western banks and speculators, and its army and military capabilities reduced to a shadow of their former strength. More than half of Russian industry was closed down. Tens of millions were living in bitter poverty; actual starvation was rampant, and the total population of the nation began to drop sharply.

Chechnya Salient

In 1996, after a four year war which saw the Russian Army lose more tanks than during the Battle of Berlin in World War II, Russian President Boris Yeltsin signed

a humiliating peace treaty with the terrorists in Chechnya, de facto (if not legally) recognizing the independence of the "Chechen Republic." All Russian forces were withdrawn from the area.

Then, following a three year build-up of terrorist and western-aided military capabilities within Chechnya, in August 1999 Chechen forces invaded the neighboring Russian province of Dagestan. Defeatism was rampant in the Kremlin, with Russian Prime Minister Stepashin publicly stating, "We will probably lose Dagestan." On Aug. 9, Russian President Boris Yeltsin fired Stepashin and appointed the forty-six year old Vladimir Putin as Russia's new Prime Minister.

Eighteen days later Putin flew into Dagestan, to the front lines, and there, in a tent, met with all of the military commanders. He delivered what is now a legendary toast: Raising a glass of vodka, he stated that we will drink the vodka, "not now, but later. Later. When the task, this crucial task you all know about, is completed." And he put the vodka, untouched, back on the table.

Within three weeks the Chechen forces had been driven out of Dagestan and back towards Grozny, the capital of Chechnya. After a string of apartment house bombings in Moscow and other Russian cities by Chechen terrorists—bombings which killed more than 300 people—Putin ordered a full scale invasion of

---

4. Between 1991 and 1992 the nation of Yugoslavia was broken up into seven mini-states.

Chechnya. This decision was preceded by a meeting with all of the former Russian Prime Ministers, including Viktor Chernomyrdin, Sergei Kirilenko, Yevgeny Primakov, and Sergei Stepashin, where all of them opposed the invasion. Putin listened—and then rejected their advice. Putin vowed that he was determined to "go to the source."

Speaking later of these events, Vladimir Putin reflected upon his thinking at that time:

> We will never have another chance to save the country. ... We will stop the demise of Russia.
> If we don't put an immediate end to this, Russia will cease to exist. It is a question of preventing the collapse of the country.
> It is the only option. ... I will go to the end.[5]

Going to the Source

If Chechnya were lost, Russia would be lost. Saudi-sponsored Wahhabist organizations were firmly established in Chechnya by the mid-1990s, and from Chechnya, terrorists were being deployed to many other regions to carry out attacks and to create "new Chechnyas." There are nine autonomous Russian republics in the area of the Caucasus, all of them with sizable, even majority, Muslim populations. To "leave Chechnya alone," as many then proposed, would have led to more terrorist atrocities and cascading breakaway scenarios in which other republics declared their independence from Russia.[6]

On Dec. 31, 1999 Boris Yeltsin resigned as the President of Russia and Vladimir Putin was sworn in as Acting President. Immediately after the ceremony, on New Year's Eve, Putin flew to the combat zone in Chechnya. His helicopter was shelled and had to turn back. He commandeered an automobile and drove all night until he reached the troops.

Grozny, the capital of Chechnya, was captured by Russian forces in 2002, but fighting continued, and Russia did not declare victory until 2009. During those years additional terrorist attacks were carried out against Russia citizens. On Oct. 23, 2002, 40 to 50 armed Chechens took 850 hostages at the Dubrovka

---

5. See the documentary on Putin by Vladimir Solovyov, at http://www.liveleak.com/view?i=c7f_1430284031

6. Lyndon LaRouche has already identified the plot to destabilize and break up Russia through deployments along its southern border, in his historic *Storm Over Asia* video of 1999. See https://www.youtube.com/watch?v=-695NtUNSII

RIA Novosti

Two Russian soldiers in a trench during the siege of Leningrad, which lasted from Sept. 8, 1941 to Jan. 27, 1944.

Theater in Moscow. After a two-and-a-half day siege and the execution of two female hostages, the theater was stormed by special forces, during which 130 of the hostages were killed. On Sept. 1, 2004, Chechen terrorists occupied a school in Beslan, North Ossetia, taking more than 1,100 people (including 777 children) as hostages. After a three-day stand-off Russian security forces stormed the building. At least 385 hostages were killed, including 186 children.

III. The Great Patriotic War

The Siege of Leningrad lasted from Sept. 8, 1941 to Jan. 27, 1944—for 872 days.

The siege remains, to this day, the single deadliest continuous battle in human history. It is not known how many people died, but estimates of just the Russian deaths range from the more conservative consensus of one and a half million deaths to as high as two and a half million. And these figures do not include the one and a

RIA Novosti

The Soviet Union lost more than 30 million dead in World War II. Here, nurses come to the aid of the wounded after a German bombardment in 1941.

half to two million people who fled or were evacuated from the city, of whom perhaps as many as half or more also died. Some estimates put the total death toll at over four million.

The city was completely cut off, with no escape and no access to outside supplies. People died from German air raids, German shellings, and German assaults. Far more died from starvation, disease, and freezing to death. In the winter of 1941-1942, the death toll hit 100,000 per month.

Vladimir Putin's mother lived in Leningrad throughout the siege. She never left. Her only son (at that time) died from diphtheria. She, herself succumbed to hunger and collapsed. Presumed dead, she was thrown in with a pile of corpses, only to be rescued when someone heard her cries of help coming from beneath a covering of dead bodies. She was later wounded by German artillery.

Putin's maternal grandmother and all of his maternal uncles were killed in the war, and his mother's sister was forced to work as a slave laborer at a German factory in the Baltic region. Two of his father's brothers were also killed in combat. His father was severely wounded by a German grenade and only saved from certain death when another soldier carried him on his back across the frozen Neva River.

The Soviet Union lost more than 30 million dead in World War II. This is part of who they are. It is written into their souls. This is what Vladimir Putin grew up with in the 1950s and 1960s. But with the loss and the

pain and the suffering also came pride. For it was the Soviet Union which defeated Nazi Germany. It was the people of Russia who held out in Leningrad. By the time that British and American troops landed on the beaches of Normandy in June 1944, the Germans were already defeated. They had been beaten by Russia between 1941 and 1944, and every Russian schoolboy of Vladimir Putin's generation knows this to be the case.

The Russians call it *The Great Patriotic War*. It was not a war for communism—and certainly not a war for Joseph Stalin. It was a war for Russia. This is the reality, the life-story, of Vladimir Putin's family, and this patriotic heritage is what Vladimir Putin has given back to the Russian people.[7]

IV. The Speech that Shook The World

Described by some as "inflammatory" and by others as "terrifying," on Feb. 10, 2007 Vladimir Putin delivered a speech to heads of state, ambassadors, military leaders, and elected officials at the 43rd Munich Security ("Wehrkunde") Conference, a speech which still brings seizures of rage to policy makers in London and Washington. Representing a nation in which only nine or ten years earlier, millions of people had been starving in the street, President Putin did something which no other world leader had done up to that time. Quite simply, he "called a spade a spade," that is, he spoke the truth about the imperial ambitions of NATO, the European Union, and the United States, and he identified that the ongoing effort to demonize and destroy Russia would lead to world war. This speech garnered for him the undying hatred of the war faction in the British Empire and the United States.

To put this speech in context, be aware that it was delivered four years after the U.S. invasion of Iraq, three years after the NATO expansion into Estonia, Latvia, Lithuania, Slovenia, Slovakia, Bulgaria, and Romania (Poland, Hungary, and the Czech Republic had already joined NATO in 1999), and two years after the "Orange Revolution" had overthrown the legitimate government of Ukraine. Western moves for the

_____

7. See https://www.youtube.com/watch?v=SSsAT1v0vOc

military encirclement of Russia were well underway. The speech also occurred one year after the founding of the Shanghai Cooperation Organization and two years after the initial founding of the BRICS.

He said, in part:

What is a unipolar world? However one might embellish this term, at the end of the day it refers to one type of situation, namely one center of authority, one center of force, one center of decision making.

It is a world in which there is one master, one sovereign. And at the end of the day this is pernicious, not only for all those within this system, but also for the sovereign itself because it destroys itself from within.

And this certainly has nothing in common with democracy. Because, as you know, democracy is the power of the majority in light of the interests and opinions of the minority.

I consider that the unipolar model is not only unacceptable but also impossible in today's world. And this is not only because if there was individual leadership in today's—and precisely in today's—world, then the military, political, and economic resources would not suffice. What is even more important is that the model itself is flawed because at its basis there is and can be no moral foundations for modern civilization. ...

Unilateral and frequently illegitimate actions have not resolved any problems. Moreover, they have caused new human tragedies and created new centers of tension. Judge for yourselves: Wars as well as local and regional conflicts have not diminished. ... And no less people perish in these conflicts—even more are dying than before. Significantly more, significantly more!

Today we are witnessing an almost uncontained hyper-use of force—military force—in

Antje Wildgrube

Addressing the 43rd Munich Security Conference (Wehrkunde) on Feb. 10, 2007, Puting warned that the effort to demonize and destroy Russia could lead to a world war. He identified the imperial ambitions of NATO, the European Union, and the United States.

international relations, force that is plunging the world into an abyss of permanent conflicts. As a result we do not have sufficient strength to find a comprehensive solution to any one of these conflicts. Finding a political settlement also becomes impossible.

We are seeing a greater and greater disdain for the basic principles of international law. And independent legal norms are, as a matter of fact, coming increasingly closer to one state's legal system. One state and, of course, *first and foremost the United States*, has overstepped its national borders in every way. This is visible in the economic, political, cultural, and educational policies it imposes on other nations. Well, who likes this? Who is happy about this?

No One Feels Safe

And of course this is extremely dangerous. It results in the fact that no one feels safe. I want to emphasize this—no one feels safe! Because no one can feel that international law is like a stone wall that will protect them. Of course such a policy stimulates an arms race.

The force's dominance inevitably encourages a number of countries to acquire weapons of mass destruction. Moreover, significantly new threats—though they were also well-known before—have appeared, and today threats such as terrorism have taken on a global character.

I am convinced that we have reached that decisive moment when we must seriously think about the architecture of global security.

And we must proceed by searching for a reasonable balance between the interests of all participants in the international dialogue. Especially since the international landscape is so varied and changes so quickly—changes in light of the dynamic development in a whole number of countries and regions.

I am convinced that the only mechanism that can make decisions about using military force as a last resort is the Charter of the United Nations. And in connection with this, either I did not understand what our colleague, the Italian Defence Minister, just said or what he said was inexact. In any case, I understood that [he said] the use of force can only be legitimate when the decision is taken by NATO, the EU, or the UN. If he really does think so, then we have different points of view. Or I didn't hear correctly. The use of force can only be considered legitimate if the decision is sanctioned by the UN. And we do not need to substitute NATO or the EU for the UN. When the UN truly unites the forces of the international community and can really react to events in various countries, when we leave behind this disdain for international law, then the situation will be able to change. Otherwise the situation will simply result in a dead end, and the number of serious mistakes will be multiplied. Along with this, it is necessary to make sure that international law has a universal character both in the conception and application of its norms.

NATO Expansion

Dear ladies and gentlemen!

The Adapted Treaty on Conventional Armed Forces in Europe was signed in 1999. It took into account a new geopolitical reality, namely the elimination of the Warsaw bloc. Seven years have passed and only four states have ratified this document, including the Russian Federation.

But what is happening at the same time? Simultaneously the so-called flexible frontline American bases with up to five thousand men in each, [have been established]. It turns out that NATO has put its frontline forces on our borders, and we continue to strictly fulfil the treaty obligations and do not react to these actions at all.

I think it is obvious that NATO expansion does not have any relation with the modernization of the Alliance itself or with ensuring security in Europe. On the contrary, it represents a serious provocation that reduces the level of mutual trust. And we have the right to ask: Against whom is this expansion intended? And what happened to the assurances our western partners made after the dissolution of the Warsaw Pact? Where are those declarations today? No one even remembers them. But I will allow myself to remind this audience what was said. I would like to quote the speech of NATO General Secretary Mr. [Manfred] Wörner in Brussels on May 17, 1990. He said at the time that: 'the fact that we are ready not to place a NATO army outside of German territory gives the Soviet Union a firm security guarantee.' Where are these guarantees?

The stones and concrete blocks of the Berlin Wall have long been distributed as souvenirs. But we should not forget that the fall of the Berlin Wall was possible thanks to a historic choice—one that was also made by our people, the people of Russia—a choice in favor of democracy, freedom, openness, and a sincere partnership with all the members of the big European family.

And now they are trying to impose new dividing lines and walls on us—these walls may be virtual but they are nevertheless dividing, ones that cut through our continent. And is it possible that we will once again require many years and decades, as well as several generations of politicians, to disassemble and dismantle these new walls?

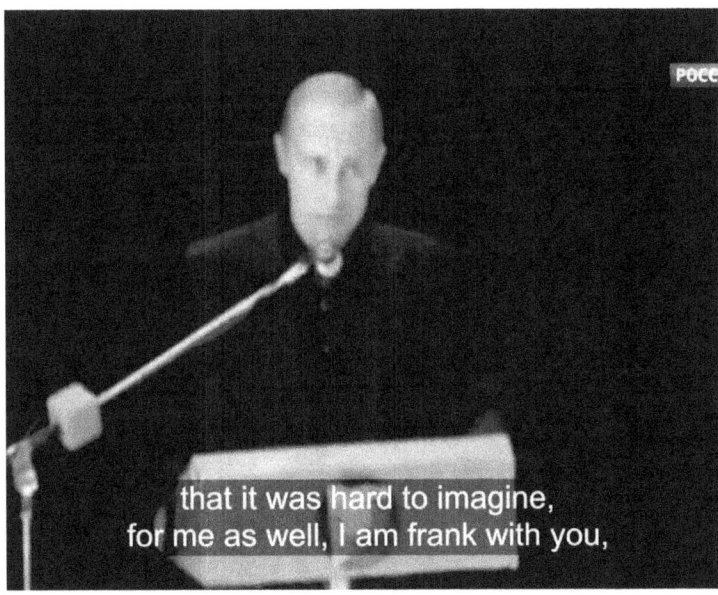

Putin faced six hours of questions and accusations from family members of the crew of the Kursk *submarine, which exploded and sank in 2000, killing all 118 crewmen.*

V. Leadership

Individual action, individual courage, when it springs from a commitment to what is morally right and historically truthful, can change history. It is this quality of creative human intervention, of "voluntarism" if you wish, which is the defining characteristic of the development of the human species.

However, this is no schoolbook academic term. It is not the province of dilettantes. As stated, leadership involves courage; it involves a heavy personal responsibility for one's actions. It stems from a deep moral character within the soul of the individual in question.

Putin's courage at Munich, much as in his stand in Dagestan in 1999, reveals this quality of character and leadership. The soul of Putin, so to speak, was unveiled to the people of Russia even during his first twelve months in office.

During the winter of 1999-2000 a human crisis erupted throughout the entire Far East of Russia. After eight years of free trade and western looting, most of the productive economy of Russia was shuttered, with only desperate black market activity keeping large sections of the population alive. By January 2000, hundreds of thousands of people in the Far East were freezing, with no heat and no coal. Industrial activity and government functioning were both paralyzed. The imminent death of thousands, and perhaps millions, was apparent. Putin flew to the Far East. He traveled to many cities. He walked the streets and talked to citizens. He fired 28 mayors; elected officials and business leaders were arrested, some pulled out of bed in the middle of the night. He ordered emergency coal shipments. He even flew in tens of thousands of electric radiators to be distributed to the needy. Putin acted—much like Franklin Roosevelt's stand for the "forgotten man" in the United States—as the defender and champion of the Russian people against the corruption of the political machinery and the power of the Russian oligarchy that engulfed Russia throughout the 1990s.

Sinking of the *Kursk*

On Aug. 12, 2000 the nuclear submarine, the *Kursk,* the most modern warship in the Russian Navy, exploded and sank without warning while on an exercise in the Barents Sea. All 118 crewmen died, 95 immediately and 23 within hours after the sinking. Even though there was no hope for rescue, the tragedy produced anger and rage against the government due to both the inept rescue efforts as well as a continual series of lies which came from naval officials who tried to cover up what had occurred. On Aug. 22, ten days after the sinking, President Putin traveled to the Vidyayevo naval base and met with about 350 family members of the Kursk crew as well as several hundred other residents of the navy base. Putin began the meeting by informing the women in the room that there was no hope for rescuing the crew members, that their husbands and sons were dead. The six hour meeting was one of accusations, screaming, crying, and denunciations, with people demanding, "Why have you murdered our husbands? … Why are you lying to us? … Who are you going to punish for their deaths?" One woman cried out, "You better shoot yourselves now! We won't let you live, bastards!" A witness who later reported on the event stated that as he watched Putin talk to the families, he had never felt such an intense atmosphere of pain and anger in his entire life: "I honestly thought they would tear him apart … There was such a heavy atmosphere there, such a clot of hatred, and despair, and pain … I never felt anything like it anywhere in my entire life … All the questions were aimed at this single man." Putin never left his chair and answered every question and accusation until the meeting ended after six hours.

VI. The Russian Miracle

Between 2001 and 2007 the Russian economy grew at a rate of 7% per year. Russia's Domestic Product (GDP) increased sixfold, climbing up from 22nd to the 10th largest in the world.[8] Average wages increased almost tenfold and real disposable income doubled. The percentage of people living below the poverty line was cut in half. Nearly all foreign debt was paid off, freeing the nation from the diktats of the International Monetary Fund and western banks.[9] Between 1999 and 2008, revenues of the central government more than doubled.

In 2008 Putin established a special state investment fund designed to accumulate energy revenues. Its explicit purpose was to direct capital investment into the country's industrial, transportation, and communications infrastructure.

Since 2001, industry has grown substantially as has production, construction, real incomes, credit, and the middle class. Major cities, such as Moscow and St. Petersburg, as well as many, many provincial cities like Novgorod, have become unrecognizable to anyone who had seen them or visited them during either the Yeltsin years or the late Soviet period. They are now vibrant, prosperous, and teeming with economic activity and human life.

By 2012, under Putin's leadership, Russia reversed its suicidal twenty-five-year depopulation trend, what economist Sergey Glazyev has defined as the western-imposed *Genocide* against Russia after the collapse of the Soviet Union. Today, Russia can boast of what no Western European nation can—a natural "baby boomlet," that is, population growth that is not reliant upon Third World immigration. Concrete steps, including economic and other subsidies, were implemented to encourage family formation and childbirth, but in the final

kremlin.ru

During a state visit to Beijing in September 2015 to celebrate the 70th anniversary of the end of World War II, Putin stated that Russia/China relations were at the highest point ever. Here Putin (center) is shown with Kazakstan President Nursultan Nazarvayev (left) and China President Xi Jinping.

analysis this rebirth of the Russian nation has come from the *Optimism* that now permeates the country.

China and Space

In 2009 China became the top trade partner of Russia. Trade between the two nations went from $4.3 billion in 1995 to $59.3 billion in 2010, and then to $87.5 billion in 2012. In 2013, during the first official visit of Chinese Premier Xi Jinping to Moscow, the Chinese and Russian leaders announced a goal of $200 billion in annual trade between their two nations by 2020.

In 2015, during a state visit to Beijing to celebrate the 70th anniversary of the end of World War II, President Putin stated in an interview that "Russian-Chinese ties have now probably reached a peak in their entire history and continue developing. The partnership between Russia and China is based on sincere friendship and sympathy between our peoples, on deep respect and trust, consideration for each other's key interests and commitment to make our countries flourish."

As the Russian-Chinese partnership has developed, an increasing emphasis has been placed on cooperation between their space agencies and plans for large-scale space projects. Despite the damage and decay inflicted on the Russian space program during the Yeltsin years, these initiatives are now picking up momentum. In

---

8. As of January 2016 it is the 7th largest.
9. When Putin assumed office, Russia's foreign debt amounted to nearly 90% of Russian GDP and annual servicing of that debt absorbed one-quarter of the Russian federal budget.

July 2015 joint Russian-Chinese plans were announced to conduct joint manned space missions, including to the moon. The announcement was made by Denis Kravchenko, deputy general director of the United Rocket and Space Corporation, who stated, "The Chinese side expresses interest in collaborating to create manned Lunar exploration infrastructure." Plans are now proceeding to solidify an aerospace alliance and to conduct joint manned space missions, including to the Moon. Russian Deputy Prime Minister Dmitry Rogozin has announced Russia's intention to create a permanent manned Lunar station in collaboration with China.

All of these developments have their origin in the 2001 *Treaty of Good-Neighborliness and Friendly Cooperation* signed by President Vladimir Putin and Chinese Premier Jiang Zemin. The same is true for the 2001-2009 emergence of both the Shanghai Cooperation Organization and the BRICS. All of this begins with Vladimir Putin's appointment as Russian Prime Minister in August of 1999. Many people today view Russia as the weaker partner in the China-Russia alliance, and economically and technologically this is undeniable.

Putin Had Opened the Door

But it was Putin who opened the door to aid China in overcoming its own geo-political isolation, and it has continued to be Putin—in the Crimea, Syria, and elsewhere—who has provided a quality of brilliant strategic leadership against the designs of London and Barack Obama. The Russian intervention into Syria has been one of those singular, historic, and unexpected actions upon which the entire directionality of world affairs might be changed. To this very moment, as you the reader study this article, Vladimir Putin continues to provide—day to day and hour by hour—extraordinary leadership as the NATO war hawks push the world closer and closer to thermonuclear war.

The Syria deployment demonstrated—with absolute finality—Putin's superior strategic thinking to that of his enemies in the west. Much like Douglas MacArthur's creation of the Inchon Landing, the trans-Atlantic war faction is now confronted with a superior mind.

Russia and China. China and Russia. This is a partnership. It represents not merely hope for the future but, more immediately, the strategic power to stop the war drive. It represents all that is best, at this moment, about the potential for future human development.

Kesha Rogers: Mobilize the American People To Restore a Vision of the Future!

Feb. 12— On Lincoln's birthday, February 12, 2016, former Democratic Congressional nominee Kesha Rogers was the featured speaker on the LaRouche PAC weekly webcast. Rogers, from Houston, Texas, is famous for her Congressional campaigns that called for the impeachment of Barack Obama and the revival of NASA. She was introduced by LaRouche PAC leader Matthew Ogden.

Matthew Ogden: To begin with, we have the responsibility to take a step back and look at the much bigger picture. We have a responsibility of leadership, as an organization, and as a movement which involves the viewers of this Webcast tonight. That responsibility of leadership requires us to go far beyond these immediate challenges, to look into the future, and to imagine what mankind can be, what mankind must be, and to take the necessary action to bring that future into being.

The recent attention to the incomparable genius of Albert Einstein that has been forced upon us by a very interesting outcome of an experimental investigation that has just had results that were reported yesterday, forces us to consider, however, not just the outcome of that experiment, but to consider what mankind as a species is capable of, and what the identity of mankind as a species must become in a self-conscious way.

Schiller Institute

Kesha Rogers emphasized that the Space program requires new discoveries, and is a necessary action by man to bring the future into being.

Man Is Not an Earthling

This is something that we're going to take up in much more detail a little bit later in the broadcast tonight, but what we begin to consider, is that the space program as we knew it from President John F. Kennedy and others, is the necessary ingredient of a mission of any civilization which is worthy of representing mankind as a species on this planet. Mankind must not be a creature of the Earth. Man is not an Earthling. Mankind must be a creature of the stars! He must learn, both physically and mentally, how to navigate that wide ocean which is outer space. He must come to know what he does not know. He must come to understand the inner workings of the Galaxy which he is an integral part of, and also other galactic systems. And, he must come to know his role as a species within that complex of galactic systems which comprise the universe as we know it today.

In doing so, man affirms his nature as a species completely unique among all species. Mr. LaRouche was emphatic that the insights of Vladimir Vernadsky—and his understanding of the noösphere, and of the uniqueness of the human mind and the human species as a whole, setting mankind apart from the animals—are something which very few people understand today, but were the result of a very crucial investigation into the nature of the human race. Coincidentally, Vladimir

Vernadsky and Albert Einstein were direct contemporaries.

We made great leaps, giant leaps, in this direction of man as a galactic species, not an earthbound species, with our landing of men on the Moon during the Apollo project of the 1960s and 1970s, and through other great accomplishments of that era. To a certain extent, the legacy of that era has continued along certain trajectories. But since that time, when the mission of man leaving this planet was a professed mission of the United States government itself under the figure of John F. Kennedy, since that time, our progress in that direction has been moving backwards, compared to where we should have been, where we should have come by now, had we continued that directionality, and especially compared to what other countries, most notably China, have now accomplished and are committed to accomplishing further in the very near future ahead.

NASA Marshall Space Flight Center Collection

Man leaving this planet was a once a professed mission of the United States government. Here, President John F. Kennedy announces his intention, to a joint session of Congress on May 25, 1961, to land a man on the Moon and return him to Earth.

Where There Is No Vision

As President John F. Kennedy was wont to say in several of his speeches, where he quoted Scripture, "Where there is no vision, the people perish." That is absolutely true today. That is what the last 50 years of a "backwards progress" have brought us, as an American people—as we've presented repeatedly over the past several weeks in this webcast—and as a trans-Atlantic system, where we face an absolutely dire economic, social, and military crisis today.

Our job here this evening, is to take the necessary steps to restore that vision, and there is nobody more qualified to do that, in my opinion, than my good friend Kesha Rogers.

Kesha Rogers: Thank you, Matthew! Well, I think what you've laid out, and also in the discussions we had with Mr. LaRouche, one thing that's important to point out is, this is the level of discussion which is absolutely critical to revive the educational and human commitment that has been lost in our society. The real question is, when we're dealing with the space pro-

gram—and this is what's not being discussed in any of the political debates or in the space community itself—this question of what is the nature of man and what is the responsibility to understand the mind of man as different from any other species, animal species, out there.

The Nature of Man

I've gone to a number of events in the NASA community with certain representatives of the space community. You have a discussion where people want to talk about innovation or something of that nature; but what's missing right now, is that there's no real discussion of the principle of true discovery, of the principle of true creativity. If you're going to get back to the foundation of what our space program truly represents, then that has to be the focal point of what is understood and what we are fighting for. Looking at the space program, one of the things that is extremely important right now, is that what has been a dividing line, is this very question of what is the nature of man. It's not about

Einstein: Library of Congress

The investigation of the universe opened up by a Space program affirms the insights of Vladimir Vernadsky and Albert Einstein regarding the uniqueness of the human species over all other species.

money; it's not about what projects are more reasonable or will actually work better; it is what is the destiny of mankind to discover and to do what has never been done before.

I love the remarks by Mike Griffin, former NASA Administrator, who I believe made them in 2006, working under the [George W.] Bush Administration, who demonstrated the idea that mankind has always committed itself to doing that which is going to leave something behind for the children, grandchildren, next generations, like the building of great cathedrals. We think about Brunelleschi or Charlemagne, those individuals who played a significant role in creating something that they weren't going to be able to see themselves, that they may not be able to participate in; but they knew that their responsibility was to actually create for the future. I think that's the ultimate question right now. What has been done in the progress of human society has been done with the intention of creating for the future.

Zeus versus Prometheus

When you remove the conception of the future, you deny that human beings have the ability to determine or act upon that future, as was the understanding of the fight between Zeus and Prometheus. Prometheus had a higher conception, that mankind can know, and not only know, can act on and create the future.

How do we do this? We do this through discovery. We do this through understanding that human beings don't have to live like their fathers and grandfathers before them, like the beavers before them. We can create new discoveries! That's what we're finding, which has been essential in understanding what the space program brings us; in the understanding of the new principles that were put forth in developing the beautiful ideas that foster the creation of such wonderful and beautiful cathedrals, that mankind not only just enjoys, in terms of aesthetic beauty, but also which have created the ability to master science that had never been known before.

That's what the space program represents! The same idea is recognized when you look at music, what great Classical composition truly represents. The fostering of our society has been, always, to take the discoveries of mankind to the next level, to a higher conception, to a higher principle of mankind. The space program represents not just a program in itself, but what is the destiny of mankind.

Krafft Ehricke

I want to reiterate the beautiful example, again, of Krafft Ehricke, because I think this gets at the truly beautiful and fundamental conception as to why we have to have a space program. It is only for those very reasons, of the conception of what is the destiny of mankind, what is our responsibility. This is what we should be addressing in our educational systems; that, as Ehricke explained, "The concept of space travel carries with it enormous impact, because it challenges man

Space pioneer Krafft Ehricke said the Space program "lends ultimate dignity to man's technical and scientific endeavors," and "touches on the philosophy of his very existence." Here Ehricke shows Walter Cronkite a possible design for a hospital in orbit.

on practically all fronts of his physical and spiritual existence. The idea of traveling to other celestial bodies reflects to the highest degree the independence and agility of the human mind. It lends ultimate dignity to man's technical and scientific endeavors. Above all, it touches on the philosophy of his very existence."

What we have to address, in terms of looking at what has been lost in the space program, is that very conception of touching on that which is human, and identifying that in which only mankind has the ability, based on our creative powers, created in the image of the Creator, to be able to participate. We have taken that away. We have taken away, through the actions of the last two administrations, through a policy of capitulation to Wall Street and a bankrupt financial system, the idea of our mission, as China has clearly set it forward.

The paradox is that we have been denied access, through the insanity of certain Congress members and people who have taken away the potential for human beings to collaborate on discoveries that are going to impact all of mankind, by denying the access of NASA per se to work with China, when we had a clear understanding that nations had to work together if we were going to address the problems on Earth facing

mankind, and that they were going to be addressed through making discoveries that would benefit all mankind.

What Type of Future?

So that's what we have to address right now. Can we get back to that understanding once again? What is going to be our direction? What type of future are we going to create for society and civilization? I think what we are seeing coming down the pike, a continued escalation toward war and chaos, means that we have a clear dividing line in front of us. This is extremely important: What the space program represents gives us a commitment again toward restoring the direction of mankind, and doing that which is our responsibility and intention to do.

Prometheus and The War Against Empire

by Ted Andromidas

Feb. 16—Prometheus is the immortal Titan from the ancient world whose name means forethought; at the very beginning of history he created man. Then, defying Zeus, king of the gods, who despised mankind, Prometheus raised man almost to the level of the gods by giving him fire. It is therefore appropriate that the name Prometheus appears at those times when humanity is facing a species-threatening crisis.

Such crises of genocidal war and social chaos have been repeatedly caused by a small oligarchic faction of humanity whom we have come to call, as did the ancient Greeks, the "Olympians." Today is such a moment! Russia, China, India, and other nations of Eurasia and Africa are establishing what Lyndon LaRouche has called, "… a just new world economic order."[1] Against this move toward a better future, the "Olympians" of the British Empire and most certainly their demented puppet, Barack Obama, have " … just recklessly escalated military confrontation with Russia" and, he now "…*pushes the new Cold War toward actual war, possibly even a nuclear one.*"[2]

Bust of Aeschylus in the Capitoline Museums, Rome

Prometheus Bound

But what is the importance of the name and story of Prometheus, this Titan chained by Zeus to a rock in the Caucasus for a thousand years for having given this gift of fire to man? It was Prometheus who created man by shaping lumps of clay into small figures resembling the gods. Athena admired these figurines and breathed on them, giving them life. But Zeus, the archetypical oligarch, hated these creatures but could not uncreate them. Instead, he confined them to the Earth and denied them immortality. Prometheus, the creator and champion of man, defied Zeus, gave mankind fire, and taught it various arts and skills. When Zeus and the other Olympian gods went to war against the Titans, Prometheus sided with the gods and thus won their favor. To show their gratitude, Athena taught Prometheus astronomy, mathematics, architecture, navigation, metalworking, and writing. Later, Prometheus would bestow this knowledge on mankind.

It should not be surprising, therefore, that among the earliest and most important plays of ancient Greek drama was the *Prometheia*, the Prometheus Trilogy, composed by one of the greatest playwrights produced by the human species, Aeschylus of Athens, and performed sometime around 450-445 BC. Of these three plays, the first, *Prometheus Bound*, survives, but the other two, *Prometheus Unbound* and *Prometheus the Fire-Bringer*,

---

1. "The Theory of the New World Economic Order," by Lyndon H. LaRouche, Jr., *Executive Intelligence Review*, Nov. 2, 1982.
2. "War and Peace—The Obama Administration Has Just Recklessly Escalated Its Military Confrontation with Russia," by Steven Cohen, *The Nation*, Feb. 3, 2016.

survive only in fragments. Yet, these plays would inspire the people of Athens to fight the tyranny of the Persian "Olympians" for another century and more. *Prometheus Bound* enjoyed a great measure of popularity in the Athens of antiquity, and Aeschylus' plays continued to be very popular in the decades following his death.

A generation later other Greek playwrights, such as Euripides, would reference Aeschylus' plays in their own dramas. Other allusions from several decades after the play's first performance speak to the popularity of *Prometheus Bound.* That the play itself was far more important to the people of Athens than the earlier myth can be seen, for example, on vases painted over a century later. A performance of the play itself (rather than a depiction of simply the myth) appears on fragments of Greek vases dated c. 370-360 BC.[3]

The very fact that during times of great crisis, especially in Europe, the Prometheus myth emerges, is a testament to its enduring qualities. With the success of the American Revolution, by the early Nineteenth Century great poets and writers would come to identify with the defiant Prometheus. Johann Wolfgang von Goethe wrote a poem on the theme, as did Lord Byron. In fact, among the greatest of English poets, Percy Bysshe Shelley, at the time of these great humanist revolutions in America and Europe, would write a play titled *Prometheus Unbound*, which incorporated material from Aeschylus' play for his own vision.

Aeschylus, Prometheus, and the Battle Against Empire

The story of Prometheus, as told by Aeschylus, would inspire future generations of poets, philoso-

Maximilianeum, Munich

The naval battle of Salamis (480 BC) in a painting by Wilhelm von Kaulbach, 1868. The Greeks defeated the Persian Empire in this battle fought in the straits near Athens, between the Greek mainland and the island of Salamis.

phers, and revolutionaries in their wars against empire. For Aeschylus, the story of Prometheus was the best metaphor for Athens' war against the Persian Empire. Certainly the young Socrates or Plato would have been very familiar with the works of Aeschylus; Aeschylus himself was famous as a hero, having fought against the Persians both at Marathon and Salamis.[4]

Athens, in the Fifth to Fourth Century BC, had an extraordinary system of government, whereby all male citizens had equal political rights, freedom of speech, and the opportunity to participate directly in the political arena. Further, not only did citizens participate in a direct democracy, but they also actively served in, and helped to control and direct the institutions that governed them. Other city-states had, at one time or another, systems of democracy, notably Argos, Syracuse, Rhodes, and Erythrai. But it was Athenian democracy, from 460 BC to 320 BC, involving all male citizens, that was the most developed. And it was Aeschylus who would inspire the citizens of Athens, men like Socrates

---

3. K. DeVries, "The *Prometheus* in Vase Painting and on Stage." In: *Nomodeiktes: Studies in Honor of Martin Ostwald.* R.M. Rosen and J. Farrell, eds. (Ann Arbor, 1993), 517-23.

4. The defeat of the Persian army and navy by the Greek city-states at the battles of Marathon and Salamis in 490 and 480 BC ended Persia's attempt to conquer southeastern Europe, and with it the direct influence of Asia in the early development of European culture. Both battles and their surrounding actions, including the legendary stand of 300 Greek hoplites at Thermopylae and the final battle on the plain at Plataea, stopped the Persian Empire's expansion into Europe.

and Plato, to greatness in the continuing war against empire. The words of this great playwright, who understood the ongoing war against the Olympians and their empires like few others, would inspire men of good will for millennia to come.

During his presidential campaign, when notified of the assassination of Martin Luther King, then Senator Robert Kennedy was warned not to attend a Chicago campaign event due to fears of rioting by the mostly African-American crowd. Kennedy insisted on attending and gave an impromptu address. Acknowledging the audience's emotions, Kennedy referred to his own grief at the murder of his brother, President John F. Kennedy, and quoted from Aeschylus' play *Agamemnon*:

> My favorite poet was Aeschylus. And he once wrote: "Even in our sleep, pain which cannot forget falls drop by drop upon the heart, until in our own despair, against our will, comes wisdom through the awful grace of God.". . . Let us dedicate ourselves to what the Greeks wrote so many years ago: to tame the savageness of man and make gentle the life of this world.

The quotation from Aeschylus was later inscribed on a memorial at the gravesite of Robert Kennedy following his own assassination.

Prometheus and the War against Empire

He seized the lightning from Heaven and the scepter from the Tyrant.
Anne-Robert-Jacques Turgot (1778)

Over two thousand years later, the name of Prometheus would once again inspire men to fight against the Gods of Olympus and harness fire. And no man deserved the title "The modern Prometheus" more than one of the great leaders of the American Revolution, Benjamin Franklin. This title was bestowed on Franklin by Anne-Robert-Jacques Turgot, a French economist and sometime supporter of the American Revolution. Franklin's role in the success of the American Revolution and the establishment of an American constitutional republic is legendary. So was his demonstration that lightning was another form of electricity. But Franklin himself is exemplary of the gifts of Prometheus.

The American Prometheus: Benjamin West's painting, "Benjamin Franklin Drawing Electricity from the Sky," ca. 1816.

Not only was the American Prometheus well known for his investigations of electricity, he was also one of only two contemporary scientists to support Christian Huygens' wave theory of light. Franklin also carried out major investigations of Atlantic Ocean currents, meteorology, and temperature's effect on electrical conductivity. His scientific investigations even included population studies.

In the 1730s and 1740s, Franklin began studies of population growth, finding that the American population had the fastest growth rates on Earth. Eventually, in 1751, he drafted *Observations Concerning the Increase of Mankind, Peopling of the Earth*, in which he optimistically forecast that the population of the colonies of North America would surpass that of England in less than a century. This forecast so terrified the "Olympians" of the British Empire, that they almost immediately began a counter-campaign, through the writings of Adam Smith and Thomas Malthus, to create the concept of "overpopulation," to counter Franklin's conclusions.

In the Spring of 1818, harried by creditors, ill-health and, most importantly, the hatred of the British oligarchy, one of humanity's greatest poets, Percy Bysshe Shelley, left England permanently for Italy. Despite great personal hardship, the twelve months from the Summer of 1819 to 1820 witnessed some of Shelley's most extraordinary and profound poetry. Besides penning such great works as *Ode to the West Wind* and *The Masque of Anarchy*, he also completed *Prometheus Unbound*.

In his "Author's Preface" to *Prometheus Unbound*, Shelley writes:

National Portrait Gallery, London, PD-1923

Portrait of Percy Bysshe Shelley (1792-1822) by Alfred Clint

> In the minds of those who consider that magnificent fiction with a religious feeling it engenders something worse. But Prometheus is, as it were, the type of the highest perfection of moral and intellectual nature impelled by the purest and the truest motives to the best and noblest ends.

Once again, the Titan Prometheus emerges as the symbol of war against the gods of Olympus. Ironically, the revolutionary Shelley was born into a family of English gentry and attended Eton, the boarding school, and University College, Oxford. Originally, Eton was founded by King Henry VII as a charity school to provide free education to 70 poor boys who would then go on to King's College, Cambridge. Eventually, however, Eton became a training ground for Britain's upper classes. At Eton, Shelley met Dr. James Lind, a friend and correspondent of Benjamin Franklin and an opponent of the king. It was under the tutelage of Dr. Lind that the revolutionary poet began to develop. Shelley studied the works of Plato, among other philosophers, and became familiar with much of the writings of Franklin and Franklin's experimental work. In fact, Lind would at one point say that Shelley "swore" to the ideas of Benjamin Franklin.

And, above all, Shelley was a Promethean revolutionary. In the *Ode to the West Wind* it is clear that Shelley is calling for revolution. The ode is to the force of revolution, with Shelley speaking directly to the wind, asking for its power, to lift him "...like a leaf" in the wind and take his thoughts throughout the world. Shelley writes, "Wild spirit, which art moving everywhere; / Destroyer and preserver; hear, oh, hear!"

Prometheus in the Modern World

On Oct. 12, 1988, Democratic Presidential candidate and leading economist Lyndon LaRouche made the following forecast in a press conference at Berlin's Kempinski Hotel Bristol:

> I am here today, to report to you on the subject of U.S. policy for the prospects of reunification of Germany. What I present to you now, will be a featured topic in a half-hour U.S. television broadcast, nationwide, prior to next month's presidential election. I could think of no more appropriate place to unveil this new proposal, than here in Berlin. ... Therefore, I can assure you that what I present to you now, on the subject of prospects for the reunification of Germany, is a proposal which will be studied most seriously among the relevant establishment circles inside the United States.
>
> Under the proper conditions, many today will agree, that the time has come for early steps toward the re-unification of Germany, with the obvious prospect that Berlin might resume its role as the capital.[5]

What has made LaRouche an enemy of today's

---

5. "United States Policy on the Reunification of Germany," Statement by Lyndon H. LaRouche, Jr., Berlin, West Germany, October 12, 1988. *Executive Intelligence Review,* Oct. 21, 1988.

Olympians? It has been this uncanny ability of foresight:

> The ability to adduce a truly universal physical principle ... to present a current forecast of *what must be also a quality of that true foresight which goes intrinsically into a true sense of an actual future which actually exists only beyond the alleged "powers" of mere sense-perception, but, which, rather, exists only within the actual process of generating a future!*[6]

Just days before being imprisoned unjustly by the current gods of Olympus, political leader and economist Lyndon LaRouche wrote:

EIRNS/Dean Andromidas

Lyndon LaRouche spoke at the Kempinski Hotel Bristol, West Berlin, on Oct. 12, 1988.

> There can be nothing more precious to you, not even your mortal life, than saving mankind from this evil and freeing society from overlordship of an Establishment which has set itself up in the image of pagan gods of Olympus, and permits such evils to be unleashed upon mankind.

At an April 16, 1992 conference in Edinburgh, Scotland, at an international science festival, Oxford University professor of biology Richard Dawkins told the assembled academics that belief in God was a disorder of the brain analogous explicitly to a transmittable "computer virus." Dawkins had included the formulation: "These are arbitrary, hereditary beliefs which people are told at a critical age, passed on from your parents rather like a virus."[7] He had added: "that 'evolutionary theory' has removed any scientific basis for arguing the existence of God, and that people who believe in a God who is responsible for the order and beauty of the universe are 'stupid.'"[8]

From prison, in response to this, LaRouche wrote "On the Subject of God." In the concluding paragraph of that work, LaRouche once again brought forth that champion of humanity, Prometheus, and the great Greek playwright from two millennia past, Aeschylus. LaRouche wrote:

> Let us turn our imagination to the Prometheus of Aeschylus' *Prometheus Bound.* Prometheus warns the immortal, Olympian "blobs" by the ears of Zeus's message-bearing lackey, that there is a real god who will work justice upon both Olympian pretenders and on behalf of mankind. I am certain that Aeschylus' Prometheus is a true prophet; we shall have an end of Olympus' tyranny soon, and that by aid of God's own agent, the *imago viva Dei* acting within men and women.[9]

6. "Man's true intention!: How the Future Builds its Past," by Lyndon H. LaRouche, Jr., Aug. 10, 2013. *EIR*, Aug. 23, 2013.

7. The quoted passage is from the April 16, 1992 wire-dispatch summary by *EIR News Service*. Dawkins' references to "order" and "beauty," appear to be a direct slap against the 1961 "informal proof of God" by the Princeton Institute for Advanced Study's Professor Kurt Gödel; that appearance is buttressed, two-foldly, by the fact that Dawkins' radical-positivist argument is virtually plagiarized intact from "linguistics" co-founder Rudolf Carnap's 1941 arguments against Gödel.

8. *Ibid.*

9. "On the Subject of God," by Lyndon LaRouche, *Fidelio Magazine,* Spring 1993.

The Trans-Atlantic System Is Finished: The Solution Lies with Russia and China

by Helga Zepp-LaRouche, Chair of the German political party Civil Rights Movement Solidarity

Feb. 12—To put it succinctly, the financial system of Europe and the United States is already dead, but has not yet been buried. The banking crash is occurring in stages, and the famous tool kit of the central banks has proven worthless, or only worsens the disaster. It is high time to finish off the casino economy and to implement a Grand Design for the reconstruction of the world economy, especially of Southwest Asia and Africa! The best approach to accomplish this is collaboration with China's New Silk Road policy.

Wailing and chattering of teeth can be heard among the financial elites: "The world can't afford another financial crash," wrote the deputy editor of the *Daily Telegraph* Allister Heath Feb. 11, "It could destroy capitalism as we know it." According to Heath, a new bank bailout with taxpayer money would lead to such an explosion of anger that it would threaten the survival of free trade and lead to calls for wage and price controls; punitive, ultra-progressive taxes—a war against the City of London; and arbitrary jail sentences. The sorry truth is that governments can only hope that the central banks will be able to gain some time, he writes.

Guardian economics writer Larry Elliott no longer has such a hope; he sees confidence fading in the possibility of the central banks stopping the collapse of the banking sector. On Feb. 12 Elliott quoted the chief economist of Saxo Bank, Steen Jakobsen: "This week may go down in financial history as the week when central bank planning died—the 2016 version of the fall of the Berlin Wall."

Nor was that the only death this week: "This could go down in history as the death of Abe-nomics," commented Neil Mellor of the Bank of New York Mellon. He was referencing the boomerang effect of the attempt by the Abe government in Japan to halt the deflationary spiral with more quantitative easing—namely, money printing—and negative interest rates, an attempt which only accelerated the collapse.

But even the bail-in *Wunderwaffe* (miracle weapon), which entails the expropriation of the banks' depositors and creditors as carried out in Cyprus, is also turning against those who seek to employ it. Out of fear that the bail-in policy will lead to a run on the banks, a chorus of voices has arisen in Italy demanding that, for God's sake, such measures, which have already been partially put into effect, be frozen.

Deutsche Bank, whose stock has fallen from a high of 177 euros to 13 now, and which has lost 40% of its value since the beginning of 2016 alone, was unable to stop its collapse despite mass layoffs, the closing of hundreds of branches, and pulling out from ten coun-

President Franklin Delano Roosevelt took control over the banks upon assuming office on March 4, 1933. Here, the New York Times *headline on that day.*

tries; it finally resorted to the desperate measure of buying back its own stock. This comes down to applying palliative medicine, which in the short term relieves the suffering of the patient, but clearly lets those around him know his condition. The Swiss bank Credit Suisse lost 24% in value in three days, which so alarmed the Swiss Bank Oversight Commission Finma that it is now demanding that Credit Suisse report on a daily basis its risk positions at market value to the authorities in the capital city of Bern.

government.ru

Russian Prime Minister Dimitri Medvedev warned Feb. 12 that the deployment of ground troops into Syria by the U.S., NATO, Saudi Arabia, or Turkey would immediately lock in an escalation to world war. Medvedev is shown here in 2013 with Mark Weinberger, Global Chairman and CEO of Ernst & Young, one of the Big Four audit firms.

The European banks are sitting on an estimated one trillion euros of bad loans, while the process of deleveraging has long since begun, in particular among shale oil and gas companies , in a kind of chain reaction among derivatives contracts such as we saw, for example, in the secondary mortgage crisis in the United States in 2007. A new crash, vastly more dramatic and final than the collapse of Lehman Brothers and AIG in September 2008, is possible at any time. The resulting collapse into chaos would lead with almost absolute certainty to civil war in the United States and Europe, and would bring with it the immediate danger of a strategic confrontation pitting NATO against Russia and China.

Allister Heath, however, was far from the truth when he claimed that governments can do nothing, and must wait for the central banks to gain time. Franklin D. Roosevelt, when he came to power in 1933, showed where the solution lies. The immediate enactment of the Glass-Steagall banking separation system, the writing off of toxic debts, the establishment of a Pecora Commission to investigate the bankers' criminal machinations, and the creation of a new credit system to finance investments in well-defined projects for the real economy—this package of measures also holds the only potential for preventing collapse into chaos and war today.

It is obvious that the policy of the European Union, as well as of the "five presidents"—Mario Draghi (European Central Bank), Jean-Claude Juncker (European Commission), Jeroen Dijsselbloem (Eurogroup), Martin Schulz (European Parliament), and Donald Tusk (Euro Summit)—is diametrically opposed to this program. They, as well as German Finance Minister Wolfgang Schäuble, hope to "consummate the currency and economic union," or, like the central bank chairmen of Germany and France, Jens Weidmann and François Villeroy de Galhau, call for the creation a European finance ministry. Behind this plan stands nothing but the intention to stick to the already totally bankrupt monetarist, neo-liberal policy, and to cement the dictatorship of the banks, which is directly responsible for the crisis just described.

Locking in World War

No less dramatic than the danger of a meltdown of the financial system is the danger of a thermonuclear world war. Russian Prime Minister Dmitri Medvedev warned specifically of this acute possibility in an interview with the German business daily *Handelsblatt* in the Feb. 12 English edition, in the context of the Munich Security Conference. The deployment of ground troops into Syria (by the United States, NATO, or the British proxies Saudi Arabia and Turkey), would immediately lead to an escalation to a world war, Medvedev stressed.

All the more important is the agreement for a ceasefire that Russian Foreign Minister Sergei Lavrov, U.S. Secretary of State John Kerry, and representatives of seventeen other governments negotiated on the sidelines of the Munich Conference on Feb. 12, to go into effect within a week. The combat against ISIS and al-Nusra should continue, however. Now, the real role that Saudi Arabia and Turkey are playing will become evident—should the groups they support violate the ceasefire, those groups will be placed on the terrorist list.

It is undeniable that it was only the Russian military intervention into Syria that created the potential for a diplomatic solution, not only because it strengthened the Syrian army, but also because of the offensive to retake Aleppo, without which the supply lines for ISIS and al-Nusra could not have been broken. The former head of the NATO Military Committee, General Harald Kujat, among others, has emphasized this, but it has obviously not been understood by German Chancellor Angela Merkel or by German Left party spokeswoman Sahra Wagenknecht.

However, whether the agreement for a ceasefire holds, and will lead to the beginnings of a real solution for Syria and all of the Near and Middle East—and thereby also of the refugee crisis, depends very much on whether a comprehensive solution, addressing all aspects of the problem, is put on the agenda.

Only if we first succeed in forcing the United States and Russia to collaborate—and Europe has leverage for that at hand—and the United States gives up its confrontation policy against Russia and China, can world peace be secured. But in addition, it is also essential to implement an economic reconstruction program for the entire region, to reconstruct not only the nations that have been destroyed by war—such as Iraq, Syria, Libya, Yemen, and Afghanistan, but also to develop industrially and agriculturally the entirety of Southwest Asia and Africa.

The only realistic perspective for accomplishing this is the extension of China's New Silk Road program to the region, as the Schiller Institute has proposed for years, and as Chinese President Xi Jinping put it on the agenda during this recent visit to Saudi Arabia, Egypt, and Iran. Were Germany, France, Italy, and other Euro-

Xinhua

Chinese President Xi Jinping and Egyptian President Abdel-Fattah al-Sisi review the planners and builders of tomorrow at the presidential palace in Cairo, Jan. 21, 2016.

pean countries to now declare their intention to cooperate with China and Russia in the economic development of Southwest Asia and Africa, then not only can the dangers of war and terrorism be overcome, but also the refugee crisis can thereby be solved, by developing the economies of the countries from which people are now fleeing due to war and hunger, so that they will have a future there. Such a humanist solution—for the simultaneous overcoming of the war danger and the refugee crisis—is also the only chance Europe has to escape its own economic doom. There is a way out only if the immediate write-off of unpayable debts is put on the agenda—whatever it may be called, a Jubilee, or a debt conference in the tradition of the London Conference of 1953, or Glass-Steagall—and we then return to a credit policy which promotes the real economy, such as the one successfully implemented during the German economic miracle after World War II.

We have a limited window of opportunity to seize the available solution, the offer by China for win-win collaboration to expand the New Silk Road into the World Land-Bridge—for a truly new paradigm of cooperation to achieve the common aims of mankind.

The governments of Europe will be judged by whether they are slaves of the banks and are thus responsible for the demise of all, or whether they realize a vision for the future of mankind.

Every Day Counts In Today's Showdown To Save Civilization

That's why you need EIR's **Daily Alert Service**, a strategic overview compiled with the input of Lyndon LaRouche, and delivered to your email 5 days a week.

For example: On Jan. 7, EIR's Daily Alert featured the British hand behind the pattern of global provocations toward war. Of special note is British Intelligence's role in instigating the Saudi Kingdom's attempt to set off a Sunni-Shia war. This religious war has been the intent of British strategy since the Blair-Bush attack on Iraq in 2003.

We also uniquely update you regularly on the progress toward the release of the suppressed 28 pages of the Congressional Inquiry on 9/11, which would expose the Saudi role.

Every edition highlights the reality of the impending financial crash/bail-in policies that would realize the British goal of mass depopulation.

This is intelligence you need to act on, if we are going to survive as a nation and a species. Can you really afford to be without it?

THURSDAY, JANUARY 7, 2016

Volume 2, Number 97

EIR Daily Alert Service

P.O. Box 17390, Washington, DC 20041-0390

- British Crown Pushing War and Genocide in 2016
- Financial Mudslide Goes On; Monetarist Tyranny Gloats over Bail-Ins
- Moody's Downgrades Portugal's Novo Banco
- Puerto Rico's Default: It's Every Vulture for Himself
- Wide Glass-Steagall Debate Set Off Again by Sanders Speech
- MI6 Mouthpiece Evans-Pritchard Touts Persian Gulf Chaos
- North Korea Tests a Miniaturized Hydrogen Bomb
- Uighur Terrorists Found in Indonesia
- Foreign Investors Are Flocking In to China

EDITORIAL

British Crown Pushing War and Genocide in 2016

II. Obama the Criminal

'The Look of Silence' Contributes to Removing Obama from the Presidency

by Stephanie Ezrol

Feb. 16—Most Americans don't know history. Those who think they do, often know it only in the foggiest way, often substituting detail, or detail shrouded in myth, for the actual scientific-classically artistic creative development of mankind. Benjamin Franklin was known as the modern Prometheus, because he dared to challenge the British Empire's Zeus. Many Americans know we fought and won a war of independence against the anti-human policies of the British Empire. Fewer know that the British Empire was then destroying India, and moving towards its opium war against China.

"The Look of Silence," a full-length documentary film, presents the viewer with a painful and candid view of the Satanic cauldron of cold-blooded murder in which our President was raised. When Obama's secret "Kill List" made major headlines in 2012, demonstrating the perverse joy Obama experienced while deciding whom to kill through drone assassination that week, why wasn't he removed under the 25th Amendment or through impeachment proceedings?

Most Americans, although cognizant of the War in Vietnam, know little about the British Empire's role in getting us mired in that disaster. Even fewer know anything about the cold-blooded mass murder of a half million to a million Indonesian civilians over a less than six-month period from October 1965 to Spring 1966, as American troop levels in Vietnam increased from a few thousand to hundreds of thousands.

Over that six-month period in Indonesia, ordinary citizens were rounded up and imprisoned. The followers of the President of Indonesia, Sukarno, the hero of the revolution against the Dutch colonialists and the

Courtesy of Drafthouse Films and Participant Media

The massacre of up to a million Indonesians in 1965-1966 in a slow-motion coup against President Sukarno—part of a crucial chapter in Barack Obama's childhood—is spelled out in Joshua Oppenheimer's documentary The Look of Silence. *Here, for the documentary, Adi Rukin questions Commander Amir Siahaan, one of the death squad leaders responsible for his brother's death in the genocide.*

father of the Republic, were declared to be communists. The army under coup-leader General Suharto, turned many of these imprisoned men and women over to freelance militarized groups to be tortured and murdered, when the army did not, or could not do the killing themselves. Most of the killers who were not themselves in the military, were either crazed anti-communist fanatics, or, in many cases, ordinary citizens who were told to either kill or be killed.

Barack Obama's stepfather, Col. Lolo Soetoro, was clearly one of those officers in the military who was instructed to kill the "communists," to "purify" the nation. He virtually bragged of this to his stepson Barack (see below). This was the environment of bloodlust and mass murder in which the young Barack Obama

AP Photo/Obama Presidential Campaign

Barack Obama's step-father, Lolo Soetoro, was one of the killers. Left to right: Soetoro, Obama's mother Ann Dunham, his sister Maya, and Obama aged nine.

was raised, from about his sixth to his tenth year, 1966-71, in a household that was still participating, or had just participated in the massacre.

Joshua Oppenheimer, the director of the documentary film "The Look of Silence," released in 2015 (DVD, January 2016) and nominated for an Academy Award for "best documentary," began filming interviews with regional and local death squad commanders and executioners in 2003. He told them he was making a Hollywood film in which they could tell their stories. Oppenheimer told an interviewer in 2015, "The production of 'The Act of Killing' [his first documentary, released in 2012] had become famous across North Sumatra—they produced the TVRI talk show hyping it in the middle of production." It documented two leaders of the death squads who had proudly agreed to re-enact their murders, demonstrating how they dragged accused communists (meaning any follower of Sukarno) off to private detention, and their slow torture and murder of their victims.

His new documentary, "The Look of Silence," follows the efforts of a courageous young Indonesian, Adi Rukin of Sumatra, whose brother Ramli was a leader of the local PKI (Indonesian Communist Party). Ramli had been brutally tortured, twice, before being mutilated, killed, and thrown in the river along with thou-sands of other victims. Adi decided, with Oppenheimer's support, to break the taboo of talking about the massacre, seeking out the killers (who were well-known and are often leaders in the community even today), interviewing them on the slaughter. He was not seeking vengeance, but hoped to elicit remorse from those who had killed his brother and many others.

Instead, he finds that the executioners, on screen, describe with delight how they killed and tortured people—using machetes to slice off heads and penises of people who are begging for mercy—acting out the murders and laughing for the camera. Two different, now elderly, executioners speak about how they drank the blood of their victims after killing them. This, they explained, would keep them from going crazy, as many of their fellow killers did. In the opening minutes of the film, an executioner, sitting in his living room, speaks about the 1965-66 events: "My men were afraid of blood. So I choked him like this (demonstrating in front of the camera). His tongue came out... I ripped him open. His intestines spilled out. Another one—I threw him. He landed on a rock and cracked his skull. He tried to hold his head together."

The film then displays the following text on the screen: "In 1965, the Indonesian government was overthrown by the military. Anybody opposed to the military dictatorship could be accused of being a communist: union members, landless farmers, and intellectuals. In less than a year, over one million 'communists' were murdered—and the perpetrators still hold power throughout the country."

Declassified documents from Britain, Australia, and the U.S. State Department and CIA present the Western involvement in horrifying detail, documenting that these western governments openly encouraged and supported the slaughter, and afterwards participated in blacking out coverage of the greatest genocide since the Nazis.

The British geopolitical goal was the containment or outright destruction of China. Sukarno in 1955 had co-sponsored the Bandung Conference (the Asia-Africa Conference)—the first meeting of the formerly colonized nations of Asia and Africa without the presence of their former colonial masters. A major concern of the Bandung Conference was to prevent a new world war sparked by a U.S. war on China. Zhou Enlai represented China at the conference, establishing peaceful agreements with the participants based on mutual respect for the sovereignty and development policies of each nation. This was viewed as an existential danger to the British Empire, and its assets in the United States led by John Foster Dulles. Together they launched the process that resulted ten years later in a rampage of murder so wide and so brutal that no one would miss the point. The slaughter in Indonesia coincided with the encirclement of China known as the Vietnam War.

Soon after his inauguration in 1961, President John Kennedy invited President Sukarno to visit the United States. Then, between July 1963 and August 1963, the British deliberately double-crossed the agreements made, with JFK's blessing, between Sukarno and UN Secretary-General U Thant. After JFK's assassination in November of 1963, the operation against Sukarno went into high gear.

JFK Library

Indonesian President Sukarno opens a present from President Kennedy.

Museum KAA Bandung

At the Asia-Africa Conference in Bandung, Indonesia, in 1955. Left to right: Chinese Foreign Minister Zhou Enlai; Indonesian President Sukarno; and Egyptian Prime Minister and Chairman of the Revolutionary Command Council Gamal Abdel Nasser.

Case Studies in Satanic Murders

A man named Amir Hasan had demonstrated while Oppenheimer was filming, how he had mutilated and killed Adi's brother, laughing and bragging throughout. Hasan and his wife were teachers in the village primary school, and several other teachers were in Amir's death squad. Amir Hasan had been promoted to head civil servant at the Ministry of Education and Culture for the region as a 'thank you' for his participation in the killings. Soon after the interview Hasan

died, but Adi then interviewed his wife and two sons.

Oppenheimer reports in a review with the *Guardian* on June 27, 2015: "Towards the end of the film, Adi also confronts the family of Amir Hasan, who died not long after being filmed re-enacting Adi's brother's killing. Hasan's wife and sons react with a mixture of denial and outrage, and the scene ends abruptly when one son calls the police (which was not shown in the film)."

Hasan had personally illustrated a book about his murders. "I made sketches to bring the story to life," he proclaimed on screen. He explained that they dumped the bodies of their victims in the river. "Nobody would buy fish or clams. Nobody would eat fish. The fish were eating human bodies."

When the Hasan family was presented, in their own living room, with Amir Hasan's taped boasting of these killings and his book about it, the sons begged for silence: "Everyone around here is friends. Even if their parents were killed, we're all good friends. Now the wound is open. Because Joshua [Oppenheimer] makes this film and my father wrote this book—otherwise, you wouldn't know me, right?"

Adi answers, "Of course I knew. I knew all about this family. All the victims' families know who the killers are. But that doesn't mean we want revenge." Hasan's sons exclaim, "Enough! My mom is ill, and this will traumatize her. Forget the past. Let's all get along like the military dictatorship taught us." This segment of the film closes with Hasan's son saying, "I welcomed you here Joshua, but I don't like you any more." Not explicit, but palpably there, was the threat to Adi Rukin and the entire film crew.

This captures the environment of Barack Obama's upbringing.

Obama, a Satanic Personality

Barack Obama's 18-year-old mother Ann Dunham left Hawaii for Seattle with her month-old infant Barack at the insistence of her mother, to get to a safe place, away from the polygamist and wife abuser Barack Obama, Sr. Ann Dunham later returned to Hawaii's East-West Center and hooked up with 27-year-old Indonesian graduate student Lolo Soetoro (aka Soetoro Martodihardjo) towards the beginning of 1964. Indonesia was then at war with the British Empire. Soetoro and his family felt threatened by President Sukarno. Obama's 2012 biographer David Maraniss reports: "While Sukarno was still in power, Lolo Soetoro worried that he would be dealt with harshly by leftists if he returned to Indonesia. He was anything but a radical—was moderate and cautious, looking to conserve what his family had attained, fearing change."

After the October 1965 coup deposed Sukarno, Indonesia was a scene of mass death, perpetrated in the name of fighting communism and ending the rule of Sukarno. Even after the rate of murder decreased, Indonesians were held in hellish detention and Nazi-style work camps for more than a decade. Obama's stepfather, however, was not one of those killed or imprisoned.

Lolo Soetoro, by all accounts, strongly identified with the 1965-66 Satanic murders and burning down of homes in Indonesia. The evidence from Obama himself indicates that his stepfather not only observed, but participated in the killings. Barack Obama reports, in glowing terms, of the lessons he learned from Lolo in Indonesia in his 1995 autobiography.

I realized that I had never heard him talk about what he was feeling. I had never seen him really

Barack Obama

angry or sad. He seemed to inhabit a world of hard surfaces and well-defined thoughts. A queer notion suddenly sprang into my head.

"Have you ever seen a man killed?" I asked him.

"Have you?" I asked again.

"Yes," he said.

"Was it bloody?"

"Yes."

I thought for a moment. "Why was the man killed? The one you saw?"

"Because he was weak."

"That's all?"

Lolo shrugged and rolled his pant leg back down. "That's usually enough. Men take advantage of weakness in other men. They're just like countries in that way. The strong man takes the weak man's land. He makes the weak man work in the fields. If the weak man's woman is pretty, the strong man will take her." He paused to take another sip of water, then asked, "Which would you rather be?"

I didn't answer, and Lolo squinted up at the sky. "Better to be strong," he said finally, rising to this feet. "If you can't be strong, be clever and make peace with someone who's strong."

Lyndon LaRouche has boldly reminded us, the American people, "Obama is a Satanic figure. And this comes from this stepfather: the stepfather trained Obama! Obama was and remains a mass killer, by his nature. The problem is, Obama is an evil person. To the best of my knowledge, he was raised to become an evil person as a child. If you look at the history of Obama's family and look at him as a young boy, talking about his stepfather, there—this guy was absolutely evil. And Obama has been absolutely evil, in the full record of his Presidency. And that guy should have been thrown out of office before he got in there."

Oppenheimer's film, artfully using the method of a series of case studies, is a useful contribution to ending the nightmare of evil and mass murder to which Americans and so many others are now being subjected.

Obama Kills Again: The Case of HSBC

by Jeffrey and Michele Steinberg

Feb. 15—A novel civil lawsuit, filed recently in the Federal District Court for the Southern District of Texas, holds HSBC responsible for scores of murders, including of U.S. Federal agents and U.S. consular officials, that were carried out by Mexico's violent drug cartels. HSBC, formerly the Hong Kong and Shanghai Banking Corporation, was the original British Crown chartered bank for laundering opium proceeds during the time of the Nineteenth Century British Opium Wars against China.

A 2012 U.S. Senate Permanent Investigations Subcommittee report thoroughly documented the role of HSBC as the number one money-laundering bank for the Mexican and Colombian drug cartels. The civil lawsuit holds HSBC accountable as an integral part of that international drug and murder apparatus.

Were it not for the Obama Administration's policy of "too big to jail," HSBC would have had its charter to do business in the United States cancelled immediately after the release of the Senate investigation, and top executives would have been thrown in jail as part of a narcotics racketeering prosecution. But under a top-down Obama Administration policy, HSBC got away, literally, with murder. Instead of hard jail time for top executives and a loss of all authority to operate in the United States, HSBC got a Deferred Prosecution deal with the Department of Justice, brokered by the current U.S. Attorney General, Loretta Lynch.

Murder, Inc. has been given a free hand to spread dope, to murder, and to launder the trillions of dollars in profit through Federally chartered banks, like the London-headquartered HSBC. This may be Barack Obama's biggest mass kill of all.

Obama Kills Americans

The United States is in the midst of a heroin epidemic. Every day in 2013, more than 120 Americans—many of them young—died of drug overdoses, which is nothing but a form of suicide borne of despair, desperation, and hopelessness. That's to say that every 12 minutes, one American died needlessly of a self-inflicted overdose, most of them from heroin or pharmaceutical opioids, either prescribed or bought on the black market. Where is the deadly heroin coming from? How is it spread throughout the United States? Who is financing the vast distribution networks that rakes in hundreds of billions of dollars a year?

Official White House Photo by Pete Souza

Notorious British drug-money laundering bank HSBC got a Deferred Prosecution deal with the Obama Department of Justice, brokered by U.S. Attorney General Loretta Lynch, shown here with Obama.

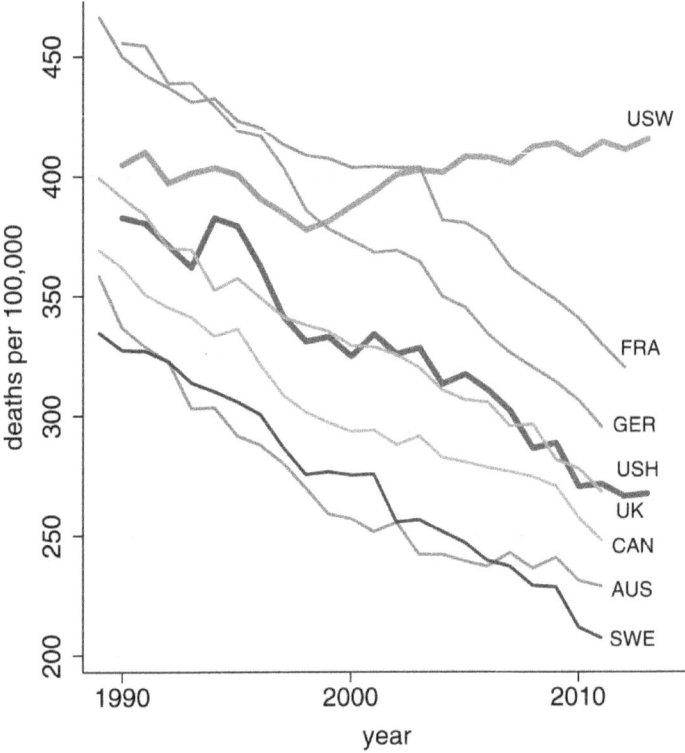

Proceedings of the National Academy of Sciences

The shocking rise of mortality rates among U.S. White non-Hispanics (USW), ages 45-54, shown in the study "Rising morbidity and mortality in midlife among white non-Hispanic Americans in the 21st century" by Anne Case and Angus Deaton, published in the Proceedings of the National Academy of Sciences. These rates are compared with U.S. Hispanics (USH), and six comparison countries: France (FRA), Germany (GER), the United Kingdom (UK), Canada (CAN), Australia (AUG), and Sweden (SWE). The full report can be found here.

Those are questions that the American people are not supposed to ask, or to know the answers to. That's where HSBC comes in, and that's why, up to this very moment, the practices of HSBC in violating money-laundering laws are being kept secret by order of the President of the United States and his hand-picked Attorney General, Loretta Lynch, the very U.S. Attorney from the Eastern District of New York who made the deal to give HSBC a free pass for the murders its drug-trafficking clients had carried out.

A late-2015 Drug Enforcement Administration (DEA) report on the National Drug Threat Assessment, showed what's been done to the working population of the United States over the course of the Bush and Obama Presidencies. The document reported that drug-related deaths had risen to become the leading cause of injury death in the United States. More than firearms;

more than car accidents. And in 2013 alone, the United States lost 46,470 people to drug overdoses.

In 2013 there were 169,000 new users of heroin; many of them very young. Between 2013 and 2014, the rate of current heroin use—in other words, people who used heroin in the past 30 days rose—by 51%. Between 2007 and 2013—or in other words, during the course of Obama's Presidency—the addiction to heroin rose 150%; and the deaths by overdose of heroin more than tripled. See *EIR*, Vol. 43, No. 5, Jan. 29, 2016.

The Civil Suit: A Turning Point

When presented with these developments, Lyndon LaRouche responded by asking: "Why didn't we, as a nation, respond years back, and take action to stop this from happening? How did people get set up to accept the economic policies of destruction of science, of industry, along with endless bail-outs of Wall Street? How were we induced to submit to do this to ourselves?"

If Americans take up LaRouche's challenge to shut down Wall Street, the self-inflicted death of our nation would be reversed.

The HSBC case shows Wall Street is Murder, Inc. It is a cancer that must be removed,

In 2009, just after Obama was inaugurated, Antonio Maria Costa, then head of the UN Office on Drugs and Crime, made a statement that been a hallmark of the LaRouche movement since the 1970s when *EIR* first published *Dope, Inc.: Britain's Opium War against America*. Costa revealed that in the aftermath of the 2008 meltdown of Wall Street and the trans-Atlantic financial system and subsequent bailouts, the only thing that kept the international financial system afloat was the infusion of drug money—the only cash available, from the world's biggest cash business.

And HSBC was the biggest of them all, according to the 2012 Senate investigation and the Deferred Prosecution Agreement itself. Exactly as *Dope, Inc.* had documented, based on studying a century of British Empire opium trade.

Obama did nothing to stop it.

But now, on Feb. 9, a heroic action by victims of the Mexican drug cartels' brutality has opened the door to justice through a civil suit entitled Zapata vs. HSBC, filed in U.S. Federal Court in the Southern District of

Aftermath of a drug cartel shootout in Nogales, Mexico, 2010

activities, the HSBC Defendants (collectively HSBC)—a global network of international financial institutions—knowingly provided continuous and systematic material support to the cartels and their acts of terrorism by laundering billions of dollars for them. Over the course of the Twenty-first Century, the Mexican drug cartels ... have risen as the greatest single threat to Mexican national security and one of the greatest threats to the United States. ...

"The ability to conceal the source of their illicit proceeds and gain access to the international financial system is vital to the existence of the drug cartels and their ability to execute widespread acts of terrorism. Money laundering is the lifeblood of the Mexican drug cartels."

In reality, the reverse might be more true—drug money laundering may well be lifeblood of the Wall Street financial system.

Texas, Brownsville Division. The chilling complaint's Plaintiffs are members of four American families: the Zapata family, the Avila family, the Redelfs family, and the Morales family, who had one or more members murdered, tortured and/or mutilated by the Mexican drug cartels. It lays out the unspeakable crimes and the role of HSBC in detail and demands a jury trial so that the bank, its officers, and its global affiliates don't escape public scrutiny.

One of the lead attorneys in *Zapata vs. HSBC* is Richard Elias, a former Assistant U.S. Attorney, who is no stranger to the practices of the "too big to fail" banks. He is credited with uncovering some of the fraudulent mortgage securities practices by JP Morgan Chase. Elias drafted the civil suit in a case against that and other banks. The Justice Department settled for more than $128 billion in fines from the banks—but not a single banker went to jail.

Plaintiffs in *Zapata vs. HSBC* are dealing with even bigger crimes—torture and murder. They hope that Elias's knowledge will lead to justice and they want a public jury trial. The complaint says:

"This is an action brought by American victims of horrific acts of international terrorism committed by some of the most powerful and ruthless of Mexico's drug cartels—the Sinaloa, Juárez, and Los Zetas cartels. For the decade leading up to the attacks at issue, and with full knowledge of the drug cartels' terroristic

Nothing New Under the Sun

Since the heyday of the British Opium War against China, the monarchy's boast has been, "the sun never set on the British Empire." With its control of Obama and George W. Bush, two presidents in succession, that is all too true.

In 2013, HSBC whistleblower John Cruz, a witness to HSBC's violations of Federal law, was interviewed by the U.S. Senate which was investigating Obama's Attorney General nominee Lynch for letting HSBC off the hook. The Senate did nothing.

Again, Lyndon LaRouche is asking you, the citizen, directly, "Why didn't we, as a nation, respond years back, and take action to stop this from happening?"

In 1977-78, when HSBC, then still using its Opium War official name, the Bank of Hong Kong and Shanghai, petitioned to take over Marine Midland Bank,— a New York State chartered bank. Muriel Siebert, then Superintendent of Banks for the state, opposed the move. She was also a fervent supporter of the bank-separation laws to prevent the merger of saving

United Kingdom Daily Mail

Obama Administration lets HSBC off with a small fine, relative to the amounts laundered.

banks with investment speculators—the Glass Steagall laws.

To get around the New York law and ruling, the U.S. Federal Reserve granted Marine Midland's request for a federal charter. *EIR* and the LaRouche movement fought a pitched political campaign to stop HongShang's move into the United States. The banking move was an "opium war against America," and *EIR* met with the Fed in Washington to stop the deal.

HongShang told the Fed that it had gotten out of the opium trade banking business in the 1940s. A patent lie.

Out of the battle against HongShang came the ground-breaking book, *Dope, Inc.* that proved there can be no drug-trafficking without its engine—laundered money.

The collusion today between British asset Obama and London's HSBC is staggering.

Part of Lynch's sweetheart deal with HSBC was that a Justice Dept. appointed "Monitor" —chosen from a list supplied by HSBC—would oversee bank's strict compliance with anti-money laundering laws. The report is to be kept completely secret—even if violations are found. But, a lawsuit in New York's Eastern District Federal Court brought by an aggrieved mortgage-holder, is demanding that the moni-

tor's report be made public. In January, Federal Judge John Gleeson ordered the release of the report. Immediately, the Justice Department and HSBC joined forces to fight the release and keep the report secret.

No wonder there is such collusion. HSBC's Chief Legal office is Stuart A. Levey, the Bush-Obama Treasury Under Secretary for Terrorism and Financial Intelligence—the first person to ever hold that post, which was created after the 9/11 terrorist attack organized by the British Empire's Kingdom of Saudi Arabia. Levey served Obama till 2011. He joined HSBC the next year.

These unprecedented civil lawsuits are an opportunity, only if the American people wake up. This time, listen to LaRouche. Join the battle against Wall Street and fight for the future, for what it really means to be human. It could be the last chance for the human race.

Gretchen Small and George Canning contributed research for this story.